COOK Indian
with confidence

Foolproof
Indian
Recipes

TANU VARMA

Dedicated to my Mumma, my best friend,
my counselor and my inspiration.

Though you left me 6 years ago, you are still with
me in the form of the life values and the passion
for cooking that I have inherited from you.

Introduction

Hi! I am Tanu, a food blogger and a cookery teacher. I had a special interest in cooking since childhood which turned into a passion as I grew up. After spending 15 years in the teaching profession, I decided to combine the 2 passions of my life - teaching and cooking. Therefore, I became a cookery teacher and came up with a food blog (tanusrecipes.com). When I was teaching, I had colleagues who loved Indian food but they would find it too complicated to cook. They used to feel intimidated by the variety of spices used in Indian cooking. So the only choice they had was to eat at an Indian restaurant or make use of a ready curry paste if at all they wanted to cook it themselves. However, nothing can match the taste and satisfaction of an Indian dish cooked at home.

Cook Indian with Confidence is my attempt to help you cook Indian dishes with confidence at the comfort of your home without relying on restaurants or ready curry pastes to satisfy your cravings. I promise you that if you follow the recipes to the hilt, you can expect plenty of compliments to come your way. To help those like my colleagues who feel intimidated with spices, I have provided a section - Know Your Spices (page 9).

All the recipes in this book have been tried and tested not only by myself but also by those who attend my online cookery classes. I hope you enjoy making these recipes as much as I enjoyed testing, photographing and writing them for you!

Feel free to get in touch with me if you have any questions regarding any of the recipes and also to let me know how they turned out. I would love to see your creations, please share the photos of recipes tried by you from this book.

Enjoy Cooking!

Tanu

 tanu@tanusrecipes.com

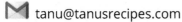 Cook Indian with confidence

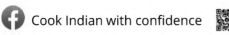 instagram.com/cook_indian_with_confidence/

As Featured on Colors TV UK

Contents

Snacks & Starters

Accompaniments

Desserts

Know Your Spices

GROUND SPICES

Turmeric Powder: It is a bright yellow spice powder that comes from the root of a plant, Curcuma Longa. Turmeric powder is prepared by grinding the dried roots of this plant. It imparts a bright yellow colour and an earthy flavour to the dishes. It is known to have several health benefits.

Coriander Powder: It is a very aromatic spice used in most curries and for marinating meats. It is prepared by dry roasting & grinding the coriander seeds. All parts of the coriander plant are edible, the whole as well as ground seeds are used as a spice and the leaves along with the stalk are very commonly used as a herb in most Indian dishes.

Cumin Powder: It is prepared by grinding whole cumin seeds into a powder. Cumin powder is commonly used in various Indian dishes and spice-mixes. It adds a warm and earthy flavour to the dishes.

Roasted Cumin Powder : The cumin powder that is available in the spice shelves of supermarkets is usually prepared by grinding raw cumin seeds. Roasted cumin powder can be prepared at home by dry roasting the cumin seeds on a griddle and then coarsely grinding them. Roasted cumin powder is used to season raitas, chaats and several other dishes.

Red Chilli Powder: It is prepared by grinding dried red chillies. It is used to add a piquant flavour to the curries and most Indian dishes. The heat of red chilli powder depends on the type of red chillies used. Some brands of chilli powder have a label on the packaging mentioning mild, medium or extra-spicy. If the heat level is not mentioned; it is usually a medium-hot chilli powder.

Kashmiri Red Chilli Powder: It is prepared by grinding dried Kashmiri chillies grown in Kashmir region of India after which it is named. These chillies are not very hot. They are used to impart a bright colour to the food without making it too hot.

Amchur Powder: It is a spice powder made of dried unripe mangoes. To prepare amchur powder, raw mangoes are peeled, cut into pieces, dried and then ground into a powder. It lifts the flavour of the dishes and adds a tangy savour to them.

Black Salt: It is Himalayan rock-salt which is black in its natural state and turns pink when it is ground. It has a distinct savoury flavour. Black Salt (commonly known as kala namak in India) is used in Indian beverages, chaat, raita and various spice blends.

Asafoetida: It is prepared by drying the sap from the roots of *Ferula* plants and then grinding it into a coarse powder. Asafoetida (referred to as hing in India) is commonly used as a seasoning in Indian cuisine. It is a strong spice with a pungent smell due to which it is added in very small quantity. It is used to aid digestion in Ayurvedic medicine.

Please Note: **Asafoetida is naturally gluten-free** but some manufacturers sell it mixed with wheat flour. Please **check the ingredients** carefully if you are following a gluten-free diet.

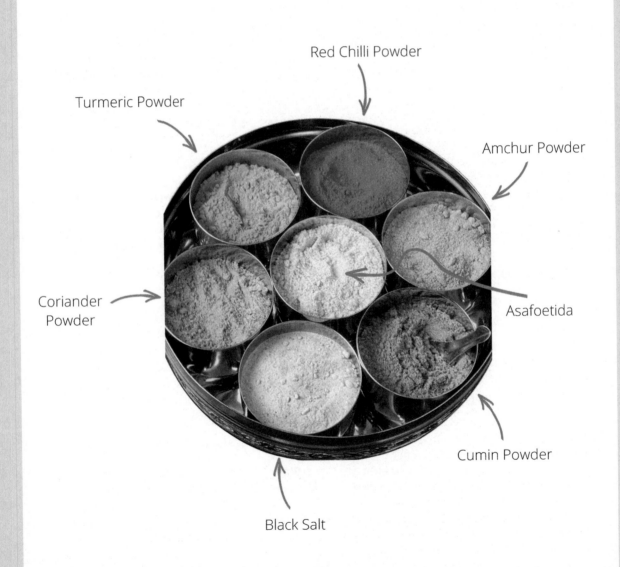

WHOLE SPICES

Cinnamon: Cinnamon quills or sticks are thinly rolled inner bark of Cinnamomum tree. They can be easily bought from the spice aisle of any supermarket. Cinnamon is used to add flavour and enhance the taste of desserts as well as savoury dishes.

Black cardamom: Black cardamom pods grow on a herbaceous plant, Amomum Subulatum. After being harvested, these seed pods are dried using a fire, which provides a smoky flavour to them. Black cardamom has a strong aroma. It is commonly used to flavour Indian curries and rice dishes. It is also used in most of the Indian spice mixes like garam masala, biryani masala etc.

Cloves: Cloves are unopened flower buds of clove tree. They are rich in anti-oxidants and known to have several other health benefits. It's a versatile spice that is added to soups, curries, rice dishes, desserts and in masala chai.

Bay leaves: These are aromatic leaves that come from the laurel tree. They can be used fresh or dried. Dried bay leaves are also used in various spice-mixes by grinding them into a powder.

Cumin Seeds: Cumin is a spice made from the seeds of the Cuminum cyminum plant. Cumin (referred to as jeera in India) is a very popular spice in Indian cooking. Cumin seeds are used as a whole spice to prepare an aromatic tempering for dals and several other dishes. Many Indian dishes like Jeera Rice, Jeera Aloo, Jeera Chicken are named after this spice. Cumin seeds aid digestion and they are naturally rich in iron.

Kasuri Methi: It is prepared by drying fresh fenugreek leaves. Fenugreek (commonly known as methi) is a very popular herb in India. The fresh as well as the dried leaves of fenugreek plant are used to add flavour to a variety of dishes. It has to be added with caution as it has a very strong flavour and can overpower all the flavours of a dish if added in too much quantity.

Mustard Seeds: These are the seeds of the mustard plant, the leaves (known as mustard greens) are edible as well. Mustard seeds may be black, brown, yellow or white, depending on the species. In Indian cooking, the black and the brown ones are most commonly used.

Saffron: Saffron comes from the Crocus Sativus plant. The flower of this plant has thread-like parts which are used to make saffron spice. It imparts a bright yellow colour and a distinct aroma to the dishes. It is popularly known as Kesar in India. It is known to have several health benefits. Saffron is the most expensive spice in the world by weight.

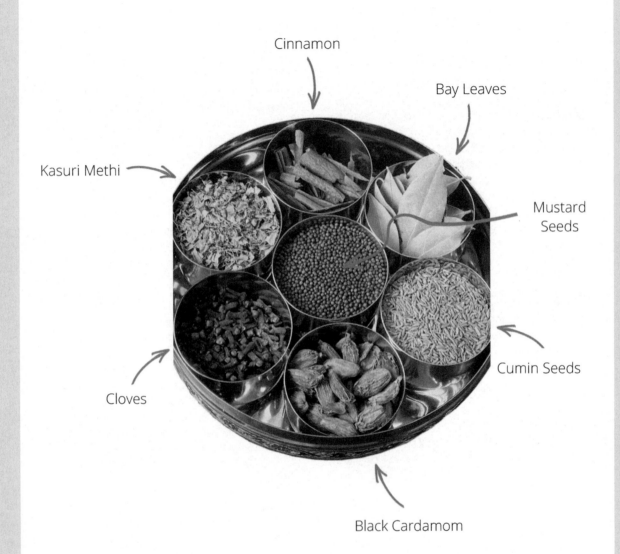

Cinnamon

Bay Leaves

Kasuri Methi

Mustard Seeds

Cloves

Cumin Seeds

Black Cardamom

Garam Masala

Garam masala is a spice-mix with intense aroma and flavour. Garam in Hindi means warm and Masala means spice-mix. Garam Masala therefore means a warming spice-mix.

10-12 black cardamoms
8-10 cinnamon sticks
25 cloves
8-10 bay leaves
4-5 mace
1 nutmeg
3 tablespoons cumin seeds
1 tablespoon black peppercorns

Dry roast all the whole spices in a pan on medium-low heat till fragrant. Keep tossing the pan to prevent them from burning. Alternatively, keep stirring them using a spatula.

Once roasted, let them cool completely and grind them in a spice grinder. Store the garam masala in an air-tight jar.

Biryani Masala

Biryani Masala is a spice blend in which variety of whole spices are dry roasted and ground into a fine powder. It provides a distinct flavour to biryani making it addictively delicious.

5 black cardamoms
4 green cardamoms
8-10 cloves
2 cinnamon sticks (approximately 2 inches)
5-6 black peppercorns
8-10 bay leaves
1 mace
1/4 nutmeg
1 tablespoon cumin seeds
3 tablespoons fennel seeds

Dry roast all the whole spices in a pan on medium-low heat till fragrant. Keep tossing the pan to prevent them from burning. Alternatively, keep stirring them using a spatula.

Once roasted, let them cool completely and grind them in a spice grinder. Store the biryani masala in an air-tight jar.

Chaat Masala

Chaat Masala (also spelled as Chat) gives a tangy, spicy and savoury kick to the dishes. It is commonly used in most of the Indian street food especially chaat from which it derives its name.

1 teaspoon coriander seeds
1 tablespoon cumin seeds
1 teaspoon carom seeds
3 tablespoons black salt
2 teaspoons amchur powder
1 tablespoon salt
1 teaspoon black pepper powder
1 teaspoon red chilli powder
1 teaspoon dried mint leaves
1/4 teaspoon asafoetida

Dry roast the coriander, cumin and carom seeds in a pan on medium-low heat till fragrant. Once roasted, let them cool completely and grind them in a spice grinder.

To make chaat masala combine the roasted ground spices with rest of the ingredients in a bowl and mix well. Store the chaat masala in an air-tight jar.

Measurements & Symbols
USED IN THIS BOOK

MEASUREMENTS

Standard measuring cup, tablespoon and teaspoon is used in all recipes

1 teaspoon = 5ml
1 tablespoon = 15ml (3 teaspoons)
1 cup = 250ml

SYMBOLS

GF - Gluten Free

V - Vegetarian

VE - Vegan

Restaurant Favourites

PANEER BUTTER MASALA

 **15 MINS** | **25 MINS** |

Paneer cubes simmered in a smooth & flavourful tomato based curry. The dish has a lovely tang coming from the tomatoes, a slightly sweet taste from the cream and a delicate aroma of the whole spices. It tastes great with naan as well as rice. This is one of my favourite vegetarian restaurant-style curry. I highly recommend trying this one as it is so easy & fairly quick to prepare yet tastes heavenly delicious.

Ingredients:

250g Paneer

2 large onions, sliced

3 large tomatoes, chopped

4-5 garlic cloves, chopped

1 teaspoon chopped ginger

¼ cup whole milk

1 tablespoon oil

2 tablespoons butter

2 cloves

1 cinnamon stick

2 bay leaves

1 teaspoon red chilli powder
    or to taste

1 teaspoon dried fenugreek
    leaves (Kasuri Methi)

Salt to taste

Makes: 3-4 servings

Method:

Heat oil in a pan. Add the cloves, onions, garlic and ginger. Sauté till the onions turn soft.

Add the tomatoes, red chilli powder and the salt. Cover the pan and cook on medium heat for 3-4 minutes or till the tomatoes become soft. Uncover the pan and cook on high heat for another 3-4 minutes while stirring at regular intervals. Turn off the heat and keep it aside to let it cool.

Once cooled, transfer the masala paste into a blender along with ¼ cup of whole milk and blend it till smooth.

Heat butter in the same pan and add the cinnamon stick and bay leaves. Add the prepared onion-tomato paste. Add the dried fenugreek leaves. Sauté on high heat while stirring continuously till oil starts oozing on the sides.

Add about one cup of water or more depending on how runny gravy you like. Let it come to a boil. Cover the pan and let it simmer for 8 minutes.

Add the paneer cubes, cover the pan and let it simmer for another 2-3 minutes. Switch off the heat after 2-3 minutes but do not uncover the pan for another 5 minutes so that the paneer absorbs all the flavours from the gravy.

Serve hot with roti or paratha.

DAL MAKHANI

 **10 MINS** | **24 MINS** | **GF** **V**

Buttery & creamy dal made with whole black lentils and red kidney beans. It's one of the most loved vegetarian dishes in North India. It's there on the menu of every Indian restaurant and in most North Indian weddings and parties.

Ingredients:

- 1 cup urad dal (whole black lentils)
- ¼ cup rajma (red kidney beans)
- 3 tablespoons chana dal (split bengal gram)
- 2 teaspoons freshly ground ginger
- 6-7 garlic cloves, finely chopped
- 2 medium onions, finely chopped
- 3 large tomatoes, pureed
- 2 tablespoons finely chopped coriander leaves
- 1 tablespoon ghee
- 2 tablespoons oil/butter
- 1 teaspoon cumin seeds
- ¼ teaspoon asafoetida
- 1 teaspoon red chilli powder or to taste
- ½ cup full-fat milk
- 4 tablespoons double cream
- Salt to taste

Makes: 6 servings

Method:

Soaking

Soak the urad dal, chana dal and rajma overnight or for 8 hours.

Boiling

Choose any one of the methods given below to boil the dal.

Pressure Cooker Method

Drain the soaked dal. Combine the urad dal, chana dal, rajma, half of the freshly ground ginger & garlic, ghee, salt and 3.5 cups of water in a pressure cooker. Pressure cook on high heat for 6 whistles and then reduce the heat to the lowest possible setting. Cook on low heat for 15 minutes. Allow the steam to escape before opening the lid of pressure cooker.

Instant Pot Method

If using the Instant pot, pressure cook the lentils & beans on high pressure for 30 minutes followed by natural pressure release.

Pan/Pot Method

Drain the soaked lentils & beans. Add them to the pot along with 4 cups of water. Cook on high heat till it comes to a sharp boil. Once it starts boiling, reduce the heat to medium and cover the pot. Cook till the lentils & beans are soft and mushy. It can take around 60-90 minutes. Add water as needed and keep stirring at regular intervals otherwise the lentils can stick to the bottom of the pot.

Simmering

After boiling, mash some of the dal with the back of a ladle.

Add milk to the dal and let it boil. When it starts boiling, reduce the heat to low and simmer for 20-25 minutes while stirring occasionally.

Tempering

For the tempering, heat oil in a pan. Add cumin seeds and let them crackle. Add onions, garlic, ginger and asafoetida. Sauté till onions turn golden brown in colour. Add the pureed tomatoes and cook till the mixture reduces to a thick paste and oil starts separating from it.

Add this tadka/tempering to the dal and mix well.

Add the cream and simmer the dal for 5 minutes.

Serving

Serve hot garnished with coriander leaves, butter and cream.

Recipe Tips:

Do not replace fresh pureed tomatoes with a store-bought tomato puree. It is lot more concentrated and will not taste as good as fresh tomatoes.

Do not cut down on butter and cream if you would like your dal makhani to have that restaurant style taste & flavour.

Please note that asafoetida is **naturally gluten-free** but some manufacturers sell it mixed with wheat flour. Please **check the ingredients** carefully if you are following a gluten-free diet.

" Tanu's recipes are super yummy and easy to follow. She puts in extra effort to explain minute details.

Krutika Potdar
"

DHABA CHICKEN

 **PREP**TIME **20 MINS** | **COOK**TIME **30 MINS** | **GF**

Dhabas are roadside restaurants commonly found on national and state highways in India. Indian food served in dhabas is full of rustic flavour. Dhaba style chicken curry is prepared by cooking chicken with whole spices, onions, garlic, ginger and tomatoes. Do not be deluded by its bright red colour, the Kashmiri red chilli powder gives a nice colour to the curry without making it too spicy. It tastes divine with naan but you can pair it with any Indian flatbread or rice.

Ingredients:

For Marinating
750g on-the- bone chicken (cut into small pieces)
2 tablespoons yogurt
1 teaspoon freshly ground garlic
½ teaspoon freshly ground ginger
1 teaspoon salt
¼ teaspoon garam masala

For Curry
2 medium-sized onions, finely chopped (preferably red onions)
3 medium-sized tomatoes, pureed
4-5 garlic cloves, coarsely ground
1 tablespoon coarsely ground ginger
2 tablespoons oil + 2 tablespoons ghee
2 bay leaves
1 black cardamom
1 cinnamon stick
3 cloves
¾ teaspoon turmeric powder
1.5 teaspoon coriander powder
½ teaspoon cumin seed powder
1.5 teaspoons Kashmiri red chilli powder
2 tablespoons finely chopped fresh coriander
Salt to taste

Makes: 4 servings

Method:

Marinating the Chicken

Combine all the ingredients for marinating in a large bowl. Mix well, cover the bowl with a cling film and keep in the refrigerator overnight.

The curry tastes great if the chicken is marinated for 6-8 hours but if you are unable to marinate for that long, keep aside for 30 minutes while you are doing the preparation (chopping & grinding) for the curry.

Pan-Searing the Chicken

Heat 2 tablespoons ghee in a large pan. Once the ghee is hot, add the marinated chicken and cook on high heat (while stirring very often) for 5-7 minutes or till the moisture gets evaporated. Remove from the pan and set aside.

Preparing the Curry

Add 2 tablespoons oil in the same pan. Then add all the whole spices - bay leaves, black cardamom, cinnamon and cloves.

Add the chopped onions, coarsely ground garlic and ginger. Sauté for 4-5 minutes (while stirring regularly) or till the onions turn golden brown in colour.

Add the tomatoes, salt, turmeric powder, Kashmiri red chilli powder, coriander powder and cumin powder. Keep sautéing until the moisture gets evaporated and oil oozes on the sides of the onion-tomato masala.

Add the chicken and sauté for a minute. Then add 1 cup of water, mix well and let it boil. When the water starts boiling, cover the pan and reduce the heat to low. Let it simmer for 10-15 minutes or till the chicken is well cooked.

Garnish with finely chopped fresh coriander and serve hot with naan or roti. It also tastes great with rice.

Recipe Tips:

I like to use baby chicken for this dish. If buying from a butcher, you can request for a skinless baby chicken cut into pieces for a curry.

It's best to use chicken on-the-bone as the juices from the bones seep into the gravy and enhance the overall taste of the dish. You can also use chicken drumsticks for this curry. However, if you prefer to eat boneless chicken; use diced chicken thigh (400-500g) for this recipe.

If you want to make it spicier, you can add some regular red chilli powder in addition to Kashmiri red chilli powder. You can also add some green chillies (cut vertically into two halves) along with the fresh coriander in the end.

I had an amazing lesson with you and really loved the food. It was such a tasty dinner. The cucumber raita was really tasty, refreshing and healthy.

Thank you SO much for spreading your lovely talent ♥

Nakita

PANEER KORMA

 **PREP** TIME **10 MINS** |  **COOK** TIME **15 MINS** | **GF** **V**

Korma is a rich, creamy and aromatic curry made with yogurt, cream, nuts & spices. It's super versatile; you can make paneer, chicken, lamb, tofu or assorted vegetables in this curry.

Ingredients:

250g Paneer, cut into cubes

4 tablespoons oil

1 large white onion, sliced

1 teaspoon chopped ginger

3-4 cloves garlic, chopped

1 green chilli (optional)

6-7 cashew nuts

1.5 teaspoon freshly ground black pepper

¼ cup plain yogurt, whisked

¼ cup single cream

1 black cardamom

2 Bay leaves

1 cinnamon stick

2 cloves

1 teaspoon Kasuri methi

Salt to taste

Makes: 4 servings

Method:

Heat 2 tablespoons oil in a pan. Add the sliced onion, ginger and garlic. Sauté for 2-3 minutes or till the onions turn light golden brown.

Combine the sautéed onions, garlic, ginger, cashew nuts and green chilli in a grinder. Add 2-3 tablespoons of water and grind to a smooth paste.

Add 2 tablespoons oil in a pan. Add the whole spices- black cardamom, bay leaves, cinnamon stick and cloves. Add the onion-cashew paste and cook on medium heat for 3-4 minutes.

Add the whisked yogurt (yogurt should be at room temperature) and keep stirring continuously (keeping the heat on high) till oil starts separating from the masala paste.

Add salt and Kasuri methi. Stir and cook for 30 seconds.

Add in 1 cup water and mix well. Let it come to a boil.

Add cream and freshly ground black pepper. Let it come to a boil. Cover the pan and reduce the heat to low. Simmer for 7 minutes.

Add the paneer cubes. Mix well and let the paneer simmer in the gravy for 2 to 3 minutes on low heat.

Serve hot with roti or paratha.

Make it Vegan
Use tofu instead of paneer. Replace the single cream with vegan or coconut cream and the regular yogurt with yogurt made from coconut milk.

Variations:

Chicken Korma: Combine 250g diced chicken breast,1 tablespoon corn flour, 1 tablespoon oil and ¾ teaspoon salt (or to taste) in a large bowl. Mix well and keep aside for 15 minutes. Heat oil in a broad pan. Add the marinated chicken to the pan in a single layer. Cook for 5-7 minutes, flipping once in between until the chicken turns light golden brown from both sides. Use this pan-fried chicken in the Korma gravy. Use the same recipe as above; just replace the paneer with the pan-fried chicken.

Vegetable Korma: Heat oil in a pan and add the chopped vegetables of your choice. I usually like to use cauliflower, carrots, green beans and red peppers. Stir-fry them until they are cooked but still have a nice crunch. We want the texture of the veggies like they are in any stir-fried dish.

Use these stir-fried vegetables in the Korma gravy. Use the same recipe as above; just replace the paneer with the stir-fried vegetables.

KURKURI BHINDI

 **20 MINS** | **15-20 MINS** | **GF** **VE**

Crispy (kurkuri) okra (bhindi) slices lightly coated with flour & spices. It's a super versatile dish; it can be served as a side-dish with dal-rice or as a snack/starter. It tastes finger-licking good in whatever way you serve it.

Ingredients:

250g okra (bhindi), cut into 4 pieces lengthwise

2 tablespoons gram flour

2 tablespoons rice flour

1 teaspoon turmeric powder

1 teaspoon red chilli powder or to taste

1 teaspoon lemon juice

½ teaspoon chaat masala

1-2 tablespoons oil + more oil depending on the method of cooking

Salt to taste

Makes: 2-3 servings

Method:

Wash the okra and then pat them dry with a kitchen towel. Please make sure, each okra is completely dry before proceeding to the next step else the okra can turn soggy rather than crispy.

Once dried, cut the top and bottoms off of the okra. Slice the okra vertically into 4 pieces.

Combine the gram flour, rice flour, turmeric powder, red chilli powder and salt in a bowl. Mix well.

Take the okra slices in a large bowl. Add the lemon juice and mix well. Add the prepared flour-spice mix and mix well again.

Drizzle 1-2 tablespoons oil on the spice-coated okra and mix well using a fork. Adding the oil will help the spices to stick on the okra.

The spice-coated okra can be deep-fried or air-fried or baked. Choose any one of the cooking methods given below to cook the okra.

Deep-Frying Method

Heat the oil in a pan for deep-frying. Take a handful of okra (bhindi) and scatter them in the hot oil. Do not put too many at a time. Fry them till they turn crisp and golden brown. Repeat the same process for the remaining okra.

Take them out in a dish lined with absorbent paper.

Air-Fryer Method

Preheat the air-fryer to 190°C. Line the air-fryer basket with baking paper. Grease it with cooking oil.

Place the okra in a single layer, avoid overcrowding. You might have to air-fry it in 2 batches.

Air fry for about 8 minutes. After 8 minutes, shake the basket and spray the okra with some oil or apply oil using a brush. Then air-fry for another 7-10 minutes or till the okra gets well cooked and turns crispy.

Oven Method

Pre-heat the oven to 180°C.

Line a large baking tray with baking paper or kitchen foil. Then spray it generously with oil or grease it with oil using a brush.

Arrange the okra slices in a single layer. Bake at 180°C for 15-20 minutes or till the okra gets well cooked and turns crispy.

Serving the Kurkuri Bhindi

Take the deep-fried/ air-fried/ baked kurkuri bhindi out in a large tray or dish. Sprinkle some chaat masala on it.

Serve immediately.

Recipe Tips:

Cut okra in thin slivers to ensure even cooking and crisp texture.

You can reduce the quantity of red chilli powder or skip it completely if you do not like very spicy.

Kurkuri bhindi tastes the best when eaten right away. It doesn't stay very crispy if kept for longer.

Tanu's Butter Chicken recipe makes exactly like the one we get from our favourite restaurant. We have made it several times since we had a lesson with her.

Stuart & Caroline

Loved the class! Chicken was tender and restaurant quality.

Amy

BUTTER CHICKEN

 **10 MINS** |  **30 MINS** |

Butter Chicken or Murgh Makhani as it is popularly known in India is made of succulent chicken pieces simmered in a smooth, buttery and indulgent gravy. This Butter Chicken recipe can be on your dinner table in less than an hour and it tastes just like (or even better) the butter chicken from your favourite Indian restaurant.

Ingredients:

500g diced chicken thigh

3 large onions

6 medium-sized tomatoes

6-7 garlic cloves

1 teaspoon chopped ginger

75ml double cream (5 tablespoons)

¼ cup (60ml) whole milk

2 tablespoons oil

4 tablespoons butter

2 cloves

1 cinnamon stick

1 black cardamom

4 bay leaves

1 teaspoon kashmiri red chilli powder

1 teaspoon dried fenugreek leaves (Kasuri Methi)

Salt to taste

Makes: 5 servings

Method:

Peel the onion, garlic and ginger. Slice the onions and roughly chop the tomatoes, garlic and ginger.

Heat oil in a pan. Add the bay leaves, onions, garlic and ginger. Sauté till the onions turn soft.

Add the tomatoes and the salt. Cover the pan and cook on medium heat for 3-4 minutes or till the tomatoes become soft. Uncover the pan and cook for another 3-4 minutes while stirring at regular intervals. Turn off the heat and keep it aside to let it cool.

In another pan, heat 2 tablespoons butter. Add the whole spices (cinnamon, black cardamom and cloves) and the diced chicken thigh. Add little salt and sauté for a minute. Cover the pan and cook on medium heat for 5 minutes; keep an eye on it and stir it once if required. After 5 minutes, uncover the pan and sauté on high heat for a minute or till all the moisture gets evaporated. Take it out in a bowl and cover it.

Once cooled, add the onion-tomato mixture in a blender along with ¼th cup of milk. Blend it into a smooth paste.

Heat the remaining 2 tablespoons of butter in the same pan and add the blended paste to it. Add Kashmiri red chilli powder and dried fenugreek leaves. Sauté on high heat while stirring continuously till oil starts oozing on the sides.

Add about 1 cup of water or less depending on how thick gravy you like. Let it come to a sharp boil. Once it starts boiling, reduce the heat and let it simmer for 5 minutes.

Add the cream and the cooked chicken thigh. Cover the pan and let it simmer for another 3-4 minutes so that the chicken absorbs the flavour from the gravy.

Serve hot with rice or naan.

ALOO GOBI

 **20 MINS** | **20 MINS** | GF VE

Aloo Gobi is a popular Indian vegetarian dish made of potato (aloo) and cauliflower (gobi). It is prepared in several ways in different parts of India and in different households. It is prepared with onion, garlic, tomatoes & spices in most restaurants and I am sharing the restaurant-style recipe below.

Ingredients:

2 medium potatoes, sliced into thin wedges

1 medium cauliflower, cut into small florets

1 medium onion, finely chopped

1 large tomato, finely chopped

1 teaspoon coarsely ground garlic (3-4 garlic cloves)

1 teaspoon coarsely ground ginger

4 tablespoons oil

½ teaspoon cumin seeds

¼ teaspoon asafoetida

1 teaspoon turmeric powder

½ teaspoon red chilli powder or to taste

1 teaspoon coriander powder

1 teaspoon amchur powder (dried raw mango powder)

2 tablespoons finely chopped fresh coriander (cilantro)

Salt to taste

Makes: 4 servings

Method:

Cooking the Cauliflower & Potatoes

Heat oil in a broad non-stick pan. Add the cauliflower and the potatoes. Add ½ teaspoon salt. Mix well so that they get nicely coated with oil. Sauté on high heat for 1 minute. Cover and cook on low heat for 5 minutes. Then, turn them over, cover the pan and cook for another 3-5 minutes or till the cauliflower and potatoes are nearly 90 percent cooked. **Be careful not to overcook the veggies** as it can spoil the texture and overall taste of the dish.

Preparing Onion-Tomato Masala

Heat 2 tablespoons oil in a broad pan. Add cumin seeds. When the cumin seeds start crackling, add asafoetida, onions, ginger and garlic. Sauté till they turn golden brown.

Add the chopped tomatoes and the spices (turmeric powder, coriander powder, red chilli powder, amchur powder and salt). Sauté till the moisture gets evaporated and oil starts oozing on the sides.

Cooking the Veggies with Onion-Tomato Masala

Add the cooked cauliflower and the potatoes to the onion-tomato masala. Mix gently. Add 2-3 tablespoons of water. **Avoid adding more water** as it can make the veggies mushy and can spoil the taste and texture of this dish. Cover the pan and cook on high heat for 30 seconds. After 30 seconds, reduce the heat to low and cook for 3-4 minutes while keeping the pan covered.

Add fresh coriander leaves and mix very gently with a spatula. Serve hot with paratha or naan. It also tastes great as a side-dish with dal-rice.

Recipe Tips:

Use a broad pan for cooking the cauliflower and potatoes. The veggies can get squashed when put on top of each other in a deep pan which is not very broad. This can make them soggy thereby spoiling the taste of the dish. We want the veggies to be nicely cooked without getting soggy.

Please note that asafoetida is **naturally gluten-free** but some manufacturers sell it mixed with wheat flour. Please **check the ingredients** carefully if you are following a gluten-free diet.

MALAI KOFTA

 **30 MINS** | **30 MINS** | **V**

Koftas are deep-fried balls made of vegetables or minced meat. Malai Kofta is delicately spiced vegetarian kofta made of potato and paneer. It's a very popular Indian dish in which melt-in-the-mouth koftas are dunked in a delicious velvety curry.

Ingredients:

Koftas

150g grated paneer
2 medium-sized boiled potatoes (peeled and mashed)
2 bread slices (white or wholewheat)
½ cup boiled peas
1 teaspoon freshly ground green chillies (optional)
1 teaspoon freshly ground ginger
2 tablespoons finely chopped coriander leaves
1 teaspoon chaat masala
Salt to taste
Oil for deep/air frying

Gravy

2 large onions, sliced
2 large tomatoes, chopped
1 tablespoon chopped garlic (3-4 cloves)
1 teaspoon chopped ginger
½ cup whole milk
4 tablespoons double cream
3 tablespoons oil
1 teaspoon red chilli powder or to taste
Salt to taste

Makes: 4-5 servings

Method:

Koftas

Combine the mashed potatoes, grated paneer, boiled peas, chopped coriander leaves, freshly ground ginger-green chilli, chaat masala and salt in a large bowl.

Soak the bread slices in water and squeeze them between your hands to get rid of excess water. Crumble them into the kofta mixture and mix well.

Shape the mixture into small balls (koftas). These koftas can be deep-fried or air-fried.

Deep-Frying Method

Heat enough oil in a pan to deep-fry the koftas. Add 2-3 koftas at one time and fry them on medium-high heat until golden brown from all sides. Adding too many koftas at one time can bring down the temperature of the oil as a result of which the koftas can disintegrate in the oil. Take them out in a dish lined with kitchen towel to get rid of the excess oil.

Air-Frying Method

Preheat the air-fryer to 190 degrees C. Line the air-fryer basket with baking paper and grease it with spray oil or by brushing some oil. Place the kofta balls about 1 inch apart from each other. Spray some oil on the koftas or apply oil on them using a brush. Air-fry the koftas for 9 minutes at 190 degrees C. After 9 minutes, flip the koftas and spray some more cooking oil on them. Air-fry them for another 6-8 minutes or till they turn light golden brown.

Make it Vegan

Replace the double cream with vegan cream or coconut cream and the milk with coconut milk.

Gravy

Heat oil in a deep non-stick pan. Add the sliced onions, ginger and garlic. Sauté for 3-4 minutes (while stirring regularly) or till the onions turn golden brown in colour. Then add the tomatoes, salt and red chilli powder. Keep sautéing until the moisture gets evaporated and oil starts oozing on the sides of the masala paste. Add whole milk and continue sautéing until it becomes a thick masala paste. Turn off the heat and let it cool.

Transfer the masala paste into a blender along with 1 cup of water and blend it till smooth. Take out the blended masala in the pan, add another cup of water and let it boil. When it starts boiling, cover the pan. Reduce the heat to low and let it simmer for 7-10 minutes.

Uncover the pan after 7-10 minutes and add the cream. Cook for another 2-3 minutes.

Serving the Malai Kofta Curry

To serve, place the koftas in a large bowl and pour warm gravy over them. Serve immediately.

Make it Gluten-Free

Replace the bread slices with 2 tablespoons of corn flour.

Recipe Tips:

If your **koftas are disintegrating** in the oil, soak 1-2 more slices of bread in water, squeeze them to get rid of all the water and crumble them in the kofta mixture. Alternatively, you can add 1-2 tablespoons of bread crumbs or corn flour. Koftas can disintegrate if they are too wet or the bread used to bind them is not enough.

"

Girlguiding Dorset
thoroughly enjoyed
their cooking session
with Tanu. We cooked a
delicious curry and a tasty
rice accompaniment.

Hannah Burbidge

"

BHUNA MUSHROOM

 **20 MINS** | **15 MINS** | GF V

Bhuna is a Hindi word that means roasted. Bhuna Mushroom is prepared by simmering the pan roasted mushrooms in a flavourful gravy. The mushrooms can be replaced by chicken or boiled baby potatoes. This dish can be enjoyed with naan or any flatbread of your choice.

Ingredients:

400g baby button
   mushrooms
3-4 tablespoons peas
   (optional)
3 medium-sized onions,
   chopped
2 medium-sized tomatoes,
   chopped
1 tablespoon freshly ground
   garlic (3-4 cloves)
1 teaspoon freshly ground
   ginger
1 cinnamon stick
2 bay leaves
1 teaspoon kasuri methi
   (dried fenugreek leaves)
1 teaspoon coriander powder
1 teaspoon red chilli powder
   or to taste
4 tablespoons oil
2-3 tablespoons double
   cream
Salt to taste

Makes: 3-4 servings

Method:

Wash the mushrooms and cut each into 4 pieces.

Heat 2 tablespoons oil in a large pan and sauté the mushrooms till they turn light golden at the edges. Take them out in a bowl.

Add 2 tablespoons oil in the same pan. Sauté the cinnamon and bay leaves for few seconds so that they release their aroma in the oil.

Add the chopped onions, ginger and garlic. Sauté for 3-4 minutes or till the onions turn golden brown in colour. Then add the tomatoes, salt, red chilli powder and coriander powder. Keep sautéing until the moisture gets evaporated and oil oozes on the sides.

Rub the kasuri methi between your palms and add it to the onion-tomato masala. Add the sautéed mushrooms and mix well. Add the peas. Cover the pan and cook on low heat for 2-3 minutes.

Add the cream, mix well and cook for another minute.

Serve hot with rice or roti.

Make it Vegan
Replace the double cream with vegan cream or coconut cream.

PANEER METHI MALAI

 **15 MINS** | **10 MINS** | **GF** **V**

Creamy & flavourful paneer curry with fresh fenugreek leaves. This curry is super-easy to prepare and can be put together in few minutes. So if you are too tired to spend a lot of time in the kitchen or having unexpected guests; this curry won't disappoint you. If you cannot find fresh fenugreek leaves, you can replace them with dried ones (Kasuri Methi) but the fresh ones definitely take this dish to the next level.

Ingredients:

250g Paneer, cut into cubes

3-4 tablespoons oil

1 large onion, thinly sliced

3-4 garlic cloves, finely chopped

3 green chillies, cut lengthwise into 2 halves (optional)

¼ cup double cream

2 Bay leaves

1 cinnamon stick

1 cup fresh fenugreek leaves (washed & chopped) or 1 tablespoon Kasuri Methi

1 teaspoon turmeric powder

1 teaspoon coriander powder

½ teaspoon red chilli powder (optional)

Salt to taste

Makes: 3-4 servings

Method:

Heat 2 tablespoons oil in a pan. Add the bay leaves and the cinnamon stick.

Add onions and garlic. Sauté for 2-3 minutes or till the onions turn light golden brown.

Add the fresh fenugreek leaves, turmeric powder, coriander powder, red chilli powder and salt. Sauté for another 2-3 minutes or till the fenugreek leaves get wilted.

Add the cream and let it come to a boil.

Add the paneer cubes. Add the green chillies (if using). Mix well and let the paneer simmer in the gravy for 2 to 3 minutes on low heat.

Serve hot with naan or paratha.

Recipe Tips:

Kasuri Methi can be bought from any Indian grocery store and the fresh fenugreek leaves can be bought from Indian greengrocers.

To make **healthier version** of this recipe; replace the cream with 2 tablespoons of Greek yogurt. Keep stirring continuously on high heat for 2-3 minutes after adding the yogurt otherwise the yogurt can curdle and will not taste nice.

Variation:

Paneer can be replaced with chicken in this recipe. If using chicken, add diced chicken breast with fresh fenugreek leaves and add 5 minutes of cooking time to the above recipe.

EGG CURRY

 **PREP**TIME **15 MINS** | **COOK**TIME **15 MINS** | **GF**

Quick, easy and delicious curry prepared by simmering boiled eggs in a flavourful onion-tomato gravy. If you love eggs, this dish is a must-try!

Ingredients:

6 boiled eggs

2 medium-sized onions, finely chopped

4 large tomatoes, finely chopped

4-5 garlic cloves, coarsely ground

1 teaspoon coarsely ground ginger

4 tablespoons oil

2 bay leaves

1 cinnamon stick

¾ teaspoon turmeric powder

1.5 teaspoon coriander powder

½ teaspoon cumin powder

1 teaspoon red chilli powder or to taste

Salt to taste

Makes: 4-6 servings

Method:

Heat oil in a large pan. Add the bay leaves and the cinnamon stick. Saute for few seconds. Then add the chopped onions, garlic and ginger. Sauté for 4-5 minutes (while stirring continuously) or till the onions turn golden brown in colour.

Add the tomatoes, salt, turmeric powder, red chilli powder, coriander powder and cumin powder. Keep sautéing until the moisture gets evaporated and oil oozes on the sides of the onion-tomato masala.

Add ½ cup of water and let it boil. When the water starts boiling, cover the pan and reduce the heat to low. Let it simmer for 5 minutes.

Remove the shells of the boiled eggs and cut them into 2 halves.

Uncover the pan after 5 minutes and gently place the egg halves with yolk side up into the pan. If they are not fully dipped in the curry, gently pour some curry on them with the help of a serving spoon. Cover the pan again and let them simmer in the curry for 2 minutes so that the flavour of the spices seeps into the boiled eggs.

Serve hot with roti or rice. It also tastes great with bread and pav.

VEG MANCHURIAN

 **PREP TIME 30 MINS** | **COOK TIME 30 MINS** | VE

Veg Manchurian is an Indo-Chinese dish in which crispy veggie balls are tossed in a spicy, sweet and tangy sauce.

Ingredients:

Manchurian Balls

1 cup grated broccoli (can be replaced by cauliflower)
1 carrot (finely grated)
5-6 sprigs of fresh coriander (finely chopped)
1 teaspoon (2-3 cloves) freshly ground garlic
½ teaspoon freshly ground ginger
1-2 finely chopped green chillies (optional)
3-4 tablespoons plain flour
3-4 tablespoons corn flour
¼ teaspoon black pepper powder (or to taste)
Salt to taste
¼ teaspoon Chinese Salt (optional)
Oil for deep-frying

Sauce

1 large red onion, finely chopped
4-5 cloves freshly ground garlic
1 teaspoon freshly ground ginger
4 stalks of green onion, chopped
2 green chillies, finely chopped (or to taste)
1 tablespoon light soy sauce
1 tablespoon dark soy sauce
1 tablespoon rice vinegar or white vinegar
1 tablespoon (or to taste) chilli sauce (preferably Sriracha)
2 tablespoons tomato ketchup
2 tablespoons oil
1 tablespoon corn flour
¾ teaspoon Chinese Salt or MSG (optional)
Salt to taste

Makes: 4-5 servings

Method:

Combine all the ingredients for manchurian balls (except oil) in a large bowl and mix well.

Apply some oil on your palms. Take a spoonful of mixture in your hands and shape it into a round ball. If the mixture is not binding or you find it too loose to shape it into a ball, add another tablespoon of corn flour.

Make balls with the remaining mixture and keep them aside.

Heat oil in a deep pan for deep frying. Deep fry the manchurian balls on medium heat till they are golden brown. Place them on a dish lined with kitchen towel to get rid of the excess oil.

For the sauce, add 1 tablespoon corn flour to ½ cup water and mix well so that there are no lumps. Keep aside.

Heat oil in a non-stick pan. Add the onions, garlic and ginger. Sauté for 2-3 minutes (while stirring continuously) or till the onions turn golden brown in colour.

Add the tomato, chilli and soy sauce. Then add the vinegar, salt and chinese salt. Mix well.

Add the corn flour-water mixture and cook on medium heat for 3-4 minutes while stirring frequently.

Add the manchurian balls and cook on low heat for 1 minute or till they get nicely coated with the prepared sauce.

Add the spring onion greens.

Serve hot with rice or noodles.

Make it Gluten-Free

Replace the plain flour with rice flour.

LAMB ROGAN JOSH

 **15 MINS** | **30 MINS** | **GF**

Lamb Rogan Josh is a popular non-vegetarian restaurant-favourite curry with very unique flavours. It's a delicious curry in which tender on-the-bone pieces of lamb are simmered in a flavourful gravy. It goes well with rice, naan or any Indian flatbread.

Ingredients:

700 g on-the-bone lamb, cut into pieces

½ cup whisked yogurt

2 medium-sized onions, finely chopped

1 medium-sized tomato, pureed

4-5 garlic cloves, crushed

1 tablespoon ginger paste

2 teaspoons Kashmiri red chilli powder

5-6 tablespoons oil

1 stick cinnamon (approximately 1 inch)

4 cloves

1 black cardamom

1 teaspoon fennel seed powder

¼ teaspoon asafoetida

4-5 strands of saffron

¼ teaspoon garam masala

Salt to taste

Makes: 4 servings

Method:

Take 2 tablespoons lukewarm water in a small bowl. Soak the saffron strands in it and keep aside.

Heat oil in a large broad pan. Add the whole spices (black cardamom, cloves and cinnamon) and asafoetida. Sauté them for few seconds so that the spices release their aroma in the oil. Do not saute them for too long otherwise the spices will get burnt.

Add the lamb and cook on high heat for 5-7 minutes. Remove from the pan (leaving the oil in the pan) and keep aside.

Add the chopped onions, crushed garlic and ginger to the pan. Saute till they turn golden brown. Then add the pureed tomato, salt, fennel seed powder and Kashmiri red chilli powder. Cook on high heat while stirring continuously until the oil starts separating.

Then add the whisked yogurt and cook on high heat while stirring continuously until the oil starts separating.

Add the lamb and the saffron strands along with the water they were soaked in. After adding the lamb, choose any one of the cooking methods given below.

Pressure Cooker Method

Transfer the contents of the pan into a pressure cooker. Add 1.5 cup of water and pressure cook on high heat for 4 whistles. Reduce the heat to low and cook for another 15-20 minutes. Let the steam escape before opening the lid of the pressure cooker.

Pan Method

After adding the lamb, add 2 cups of water in the same pan. Let it come to a sharp boil. Cover the pan and reduce the heat to medium. Let it cook on medium heat for 40-60 minutes or till the lambs becomes tender. Add more water (if required) while cooking the lamb.

Serving Lamb Roganjosh

Once cooked till lamb is tender, sprinkle a pinch of garam masala. Cover with a lid and let it rest for 5-10 minutes to let the flavours infuse.

Serve hot with boiled rice or any Indian flatbread.

Recipe Tips:

It's best to use **lamb on-the-bone** as the juices from the bones seep into the curry lending it a lot of additional flavour and taste. I like to use on-the-bone pieces of lamb leg or lamb shoulder for this curry.

Please note that asafoetida is **naturally gluten-free** but some manufacturers sell it mixed with wheat flour. Please **check the ingredients** carefully if you are following a gluten-free diet.

Home-Style Curries

ALOO MATAR
Potato & Peas Curry

 **PREP**TIME **15 MINS** | **COOK**TIME **20 MINS** | GF VE

Potato (Aloo) and Peas (Matar) cooked in a simple yet delicious curry made of onion, tomato and spices. If you love curries and hesitate to cook them because you think they would be too complicated, this is the recipe for you. It is a classic Indian curry which is a breeze to make. This quick and easy curry is super versatile and goes well with roti, paratha, puri or rice.

Ingredients:

2 medium-sized potatoes, cut into bite-size pieces
½ cup peas
1 large red onion, finely chopped
4 fresh tomatoes, finely chopped
1 tablespoon freshly ground ginger
4 tablespoons oil
1 cinnamon stick
1-2 bay leaves
½ teaspoon turmeric powder
1.5 teaspoon Kashmiri red chilli powder
1 teaspoon coriander powder
½ teaspoon cumin seeds
¼ teaspoon asafoetida
Salt to taste
Handful of finely chopped fresh coriander (cilantro)

Makes: 4 servings

Method:

Heat oil in a pressure cooker. Add the cinnamon stick, bay leaves and cumin seeds. When the cumin seeds start crackling, add the asafoetida, onions and freshly ground ginger. Sauté for 1-2 minutes or till the onions turn light golden in colour. Add the tomatoes, coriander powder, turmeric powder, Kashmiri red chilli powder and salt. Cook on high heat for 4-5 minutes (while stirring regulalrly) or till the oil starts separating from the masala paste.

Add the potatoes & peas to the onion-tomato masala. Mix well.

Add 2 cups of water and mix well. You can add more or less water depending upon your liking. Close the lid of the pressure cooker and cook on high heat for 3 whistles. Reduce the heat to low and cook for 2-3 minutes. Allow the steam to escape before opening the lid of pressure cooker.

Serve hot garnished with fresh coriander leaves.

Recipe Tips:

If not using a pressure cooker, prepare the onion-tomato masala (as mentioned in the recipe) in a pan. Add the potato, peas and water. Let it come to a sharp boil and cover the pan with a lid. Reduce the heat to medium-low and cook for 10-15 minutes or till potatoes are cooked. Cut the potatoes in small and thin pieces for faster cooking.

Kashmiri Red Chilli powder imparts a bright red colour to the curry without making it too hot. You can replace it with regular chilli powder but add less (about ½ teaspoon or to taste) otherwise you will end up with a very hot curry.

Please note that asafoetida is **naturally gluten-free** but some manufacturers sell it mixed with wheat flour. Please **check the ingredients** carefully if you are following a gluten-free diet.

KADHI PAKORA

 **PREP**TIME **20 MINS** |  **COOK**TIME **30 MINS** | **GF** **V**

Use asafoetida that doesn't have wheat flour mixed in it

Tangy & flavourful yogurt based curry served with onion & potato fritters dunked in it. 'Kadhi' means slow-cooked curry, and 'Pakora' means fritters. It is one of the most popular North-Indian dishes. It is made in different ways in different regions of India. Kadhi Pakora is the punjabi version which is thicker and served with fritters (pakoras). It tastes great with boiled rice.

Ingredients:

Pakoras
1 medium-sized onion, thinly sliced
1 small potato, finely chopped
1 cup finely chopped spinach (can be replaced with fenugreek leaves)
1 teaspoon freshly ground garlic
½ teaspoon freshly ground ginger
½ cup gram flour (besan)
½ teaspoon carom seeds
½ teaspoon coriander powder
¼ teaspoon baking soda
Salt to taste
Oil for deep-frying

Kadhi
1 cup full-fat Greek yogurt
1 cup full-fat natural yogurt
3-4 tablespoons gram flour (besan)
4-5 garlic cloves, finely chopped
5-6 fresh curry leaves
3 tablespoons oil
½ teaspoon cumin seeds
½ teaspoon black mustard seeds
3 dried whole red chillies
¼ teaspoon asafoetida
1 teaspoon turmeric powder
¼ teaspoon fenugreek powder
2 teaspoons coriander powder
½ teaspoon red chilli powder or to taste
Salt to taste
Handful of finely chopped fresh coriander

Makes: 4-5 servings

Method:

Pakoras
Combine all the ingredients for pakoras except oil in a large bowl. Mix well.

Add about ¼ cup of water or as required to make a thick batter and mix well.

Heat oil in a pan for deep-frying. The oil should be medium hot to fry perfect pakoras. To check if the oil is medium hot, drop a bit of batter into the oil; the batter should come up but not change color right away.

Drop 6-8 spoonfuls (depending on the size of your pan) of the pakora mixture into the oil. Deep fry the pakoras on medium heat till they turn golden brown and crispy from all sides. Place them on a dish lined with kitchen towel/absorbent paper napkins to get rid of the excess oil.

Repeat the same process for rest of the pakora mixture.

Kadhi
Combine the yogurt and gram flour in a blender and blend till smooth. Keep aside.

Heat oil in a deep pan. Add cumin seeds and mustard seeds. When the seeds crackle, add asafoetida, curry leaves, whole red chillies, fenugreek powder (ground fenugreek/methi seeds) and chopped garlic. Saute for about 30 seconds and add salt, turmeric, coriander and red chilli powder.

Add the blended yogurt (after blending it with gram flour) into the pan along with 2 cups of water. At this stage, the kadhi should look thinner than what you would like it to be because it becomes thicker when it gets cooked. You can adjust the amount of water according to your taste. Keep stirring continuously till it starts boiling. **It is very important not to leave the kadhi unattended, it needs to be stirred continuously till it comes to a boil otherwise it can curdle.**

Once it starts boiling, cover the pan and reduce the heat to low. Let it simmer for 10-15 minutes stirring occasionally.

Add pakoras and simmer for 2-3 minutes. Add coriander leaves and mix gently.

Serve hot with boiled rice or pulao.

HOME-STYLE CHICKEN CURRY

 **10 MINS** | **Marination Time : 6-8 HRS** | **25 MINS** |

A simple yet flavourful home-style chicken curry made with chicken marinated in yogurt, spices, ginger and garlic. This is perhaps the easiest chicken curry you can ever prepare and still tastes divine. Serve it with rice or any Indian bread of your choice for a simple weekday dinner.

Ingredients:

For Marinating
750g baby chicken (cut into small pieces)
¼ cup plain yogurt
1 tablespoon coarsely ground garlic cloves (5-6 cloves)
1 tablespoon coarsely ground ginger
2 teaspoons Kashmiri red chilli powder
1.5 teaspoons coriander powder
1 teaspoon turmeric powder
¼ teaspoon garam masala
Salt to taste

For the Curry
2 red onions, finely chopped
½ teaspoon cumin seeds
1 cinnamon stick
3 cloves
1 black cardamom
2-3 bay leaves
4 tablespoons oil
2 tablespoons finely chopped coriander leaves

Makes: 4 servings

Method:

Combine all the ingredients for marinating in a large bowl and mix well. Cover with a cling film and keep in the refrigerator overnight (ideally) or for as much time as you can.

Heat oil in a pan. Add the cumin seeds, cinnamon stick, black cardamom, cloves and bay leaves. Sauté for few seconds and then add the finely chopped onions. Sauté till the onions turn golden brown in colour.

Add the marinated chicken and cook on high heat while stirring continuously. Cook till all the moisture gets evaporated and the oil starts separating.

Add 1.5 cups of water and let it boil. You can add more or less water depending upon how much gravy you would like. When the water starts boiling, cover the pan. Reduce the heat to medium-low and let it simmer for 15 minutes or till the chicken is tender.

Add fresh coriander leaves and serve hot with naan or rice.

Recipe Tips:

Marinating the chicken would let it absorb the flavours and tenderize it. However, if you would like to prepare this curry instantly; just marinate the chicken and let it rest while you chop your onions and get ready with rest of your ingredients.

It's best to use **chicken on-the-bone** as the juices from the bones seep into the gravy and enhance the overall taste of the dish. You can also use chicken drumsticks for this curry. However, if you prefer to eat boneless chicken; use diced chicken thigh (400-500g) for this recipe.

If you want to **make it spicier**, you can add some regular red chilli powder in addition to Kashmiri red chilli powder. You can also add some green chillies (cut vertically into two halves) along with the fresh coriander in the end.

MATAR PANEER

 **PREP**TIME **15 MINS** | **COOK**TIME **20 MINS** | **GF** **V**

A delicious curry made of succulent paneer cubes and green peas (matar). It's a classic vegetarian curry that hails from the north of India.

Ingredients:

250g Paneer, cubed
½ cup peas
1 large onion, finely chopped
2 tomatoes (pureed)
1 tablespoon garlic paste
1 tablespoon ginger paste
3-4 tablespoons oil
1 cinnamon stick
1 black cardamom
2 cloves
2 bay leaves
1 teaspoon coriander powder
1 teaspoon red chilli powder
    or to taste
½ teaspoon turmeric powder
1 teaspoon kasuri methi
    (dried fenugreek leaves)
2 tablespoons finely chopped
    coriander leaves
Salt to taste

Makes: 4 servings

Method:

Heat oil in a pan and add the cinnamon, black cardamom, bay leaves and cloves. Saute them for few seconds and then add the finely chopped onions along with the ginger & garlic paste. Sauté till they turn golden brown. Add the pureed tomatoes, salt, turmeric powder, coriander powder and red chilli powder. Sauté till oil starts oozing.

Add the peas and kasuri methi. Saute them in the onion-tomato masala for a minute.

Add 1 cup of water and let it come to a boil. You can add more water if you like a runny gravy. Once it comes to a boil, cover the pan and reduce the heat to low. Let it simmer for 7 minutes.

Add the paneer cubes to the gravy. Cover the pan and cook on low heat for 2 minutes so that the paneer absorbs the flavours of the spices.

Add fresh coriander leaves. Mix gently.

Serve hot with rice or roti.

RAJMA
Red Kidney Beans Curry

 **PREP** TIME **15 MINS** |  **COOK** TIME **25 MINS** | GF VE

Red Kidney Beans simmered in a delectable tomato based curry. It makes a hearty meal when paired with chawal (rice). Rajma-Chawal is one of the most popular meal combos in North-India; it is available in most college and office canteens. Serve it with pickled onions on the side for a soul-satisfying meal.

Ingredients:

1 cup Red Kidney Beans

1 large red onion, finely chopped

3-4 fresh tomatoes, pureed in a grinder/blender

1.5 tablespoons freshly ground garlic

1 tablespoon freshly ground ginger

4 tablespoons oil

1 cinnamon stick

1 black cardamom

2-3 bay leaves

¾ teaspoon red chilli powder or to taste

1 teaspoon coriander powder

Salt to taste

Makes: 4-5 servings

Method:

Soak the red kidney beans in 3 cups of water for 6-8 hours or overnight.

Drain the soaked red kidney beans. Add them to a pressure cooker along with 2.5 cups water, cinnamon stick, black cardamom, bay leaves and salt. Pressure cook on high for 6 whistles. Reduce the heat to low and pressure cook for 10-15 minutes. Allow the steam to escape before opening the lid of pressure cooker.

Heat oil in a deep pan. Add the onions and freshly ground ginger & garlic. Sauté for 2-3 minutes or till the onions turn light golden brown in colour. Add the pureed tomatoes, coriander powder, red chilli powder and salt. Cook on high heat for 4-5 minutes or till the oil starts separating from the masala paste.

Combine the onion-tomato masala with the boiled red kidney beans in the pressure cooker. Mix well. You can add more water at this point if you like a runny gravy.

Close the lid of the pressure cooker and cook on high heat for 2 whistles. Reduce the heat to low and cook for 5 minutes. Allow the steam to escape before opening the lid of the pressure cooker.

Serve hot with rice.

Recipe Tips:

You can also use tinned red kidney beans for this curry which would taste good as well but I definitely prefer preparing it from scratch as that version tastes even better.

If using tinned beans, use 2 tins (400g each) of boiled beans for this recipe. Drain and rinse the beans. Start with making the onion-tomato masala (as explained in the recipe), add the drained beans to the masala along with 2 cups of water. Mash some beans (not all) with the back of a ladle; this will make the gravy thicker. Let it come to a sharp boil and then cover the pan with a lid. Reduce the heat to low and let it simmer for 10 minutes.

Please note that you do not need a **pressure cooker** if using tinned kidney beans.

TADKA DAL

 **PREP TIME 15 MINS** |  **COOK TIME 25 MINS** |

Use asafoetida that doesn't have wheat flour mixed in it

Lentils (Dal) cooked to perfection and served with an aromatic **tempering (Tadka)** of cumin seeds, garlic and dried red chillies. Dal-Rice is the most commonly prepared meal in Indian households. A bowl of freshly prepared dal served with rice feels like heaven after a long working day.

Ingredients:

- ½ cup tuvar dal (split pigeon peas)
- 2 tablespoons red lentils
- 2 tomatoes (pureed)
- 1 onion, finely chopped
- 1 tablespoon finely chopped garlic (4-5 cloves)
- 1 teaspoon freshly ground ginger
- 2 tablespoons finely chopped coriander leaves
- 2 green chillies, cut vertically into 2 halves (optional)
- 2 tablespoons oil
- 1 tablespoon ghee + 1 teaspoon
- ¼ teaspoon turmeric powder
- ¾ teaspoon red chilli powder or to taste
- ½ teaspoon amchur powder (dried raw mango powder)
- 1 tablespoon lemon juice
- 1 teaspoon cumin seeds
- ¼ teaspoon asafoetida
- 3-4 dried whole red chillies
- Salt to taste

Makes: 4-5 servings

Method:

Boiling the Dal

To boil the dal, choose any one of the methods given below.

Pressure Cooker Method

Combine tuvar dal, red lentils, 1 teaspoon ghee and 2 cups of water in a pressure cooker. Pressure cook on high heat for 4 whistles and on low heat for 7 minutes. Let the steam escape before opening the lid of pressure cooker.

Instant Pot Method

Cook on high pressure for 10 minutes followed by natural pressure release.

Pan/Pot Method

Add the tuvar dal and red lentils to the pot. Add 4 cups of water and let it come to a sharp boil. Cover the pot and cook on medium heat till the lentils are soft and mushy. It can take around 45-60 minutes. Add water as needed. Keep stirring at regular intervals otherwise the lentils can stick to the bottom of the pot.

Onion-Tomato Masala

Heat oil in a pan. Add the chopped onions and sauté till they turn golden brown in colour. Add half of the pureed tomatoes, salt and red chilli powder (½ teaspoon or to taste). Cook for 3-4 minutes or till oil starts separating from the masala. The masala is ready, keep it aside.

Seasoning the Dal

Add 1 cup water, remaining pureed tomatoes, freshly ground ginger, turmeric powder, amchur powder and salt to the cooked dal. Let it boil. When it starts boiling, reduce the heat to low and let it simmer for 5-7 minutes.

Turn off the heat. Add onion & tomato masala, green chillies (if using), lemon juice and coriander leaves. Mix well. Take this dal out in a serving bowl.

Tempering the Dal

Heat ghee in a small pan for the tempering (tadka). Add cumin seeds and let them crackle. Add garlic, dried whole red chillies and asafoetida. Saute till the garlic turns golden brown in colour. Add ¼ teaspoon red chilli powder and turn off the heat. Pour this tadka over the dal and serve immediately.

VEGETABLE KOFTA

 **30 MINS** |  **30 MINS** |

Deep-fried mixed vegetable balls (koftas) dunked in a silky and flavoursome home-style gravy. It's a great way to use the left-over veggies in your refrigerator or feed them to any fussy eaters you may have in your family.

Ingredients:

Koftas

3 medium-sized boiled
    potatoes (peeled and
    mashed)
1 carrot
2-3 florets cauliflower
3 tablespoons sweetcorn
1 -2 green chillies (optional)
1 teaspoon chopped ginger
Handful of fresh coriander
2 bread slices (white or
    wholewheat)
1.5 tablespoon corn flour
1.5 teaspoon chaat masala
Salt to taste
Oil for deep-frying

Gravy

2 onions, sliced
2 tomatoes, chopped
4-5 garlic cloves, chopped
1 teaspoon chopped ginger
½ teaspoon turmeric powder
1 teaspoon coriander powder
½ teaspoon cumin seeds
1 teaspoon red chilli powder
    or to taste
1 cinnamon stick
2 bay leaves
2 cloves
1 whole black cardamom
3 tablespoons oil
Salt to taste

Makes: 4 servings

Method:

Koftas

Combine the cauliflower, carrot, sweetcorn, ginger, green chilli (if using) and fresh coriander in a food processor jar and mince them.

Mix the minced veggies with boiled mashed potatoes, corn flour, chaat masala and salt.

Soak the bread slices in water and squeeze them between your hands to get rid of excess water. Crumble them into the kofta mixture and mix well.

Shape the mixture into small balls (koftas).

Heat enough oil in a pan to deep-fry the koftas. Add 2-3 koftas at one time and fry them on medium-high heat until golden brown from all sides. Adding too many koftas at one time can bring down the temperature of the oil as a result of which the koftas can disintegrate in the oil. Take them out in a dish lined with kitchen towel to get rid of the excess oil.

Gravy

Heat oil in a pan. Add the cumin seeds, black cardamom, cloves, sliced onions, ginger and garlic. Sauté for 3-4 minutes (while stirring regularly) or till the onions turn light golden brown in colour. Keep aside and let it cool.

Once cooled, add the contents of the pan to a grinder. Add the tomatoes, turmeric powder, coriander powder, red chilli powder and salt. Grind into a smooth paste.

Heat oil in a deep pan. Add cinnamon stick and bay leaves. Add the ground masala paste and keep sautéing until the moisture gets evaporated and oil starts oozing. Add about 2 cups of water or as required depending on how thick you would like the gravy. Mix well and let it boil. When it starts boiling, cover the pan and reduce the heat to low. Let the gravy simmer for 8-10 minutes. Turn off the heat and keep the gravy aside.

Serving the Kofta Curry

To serve, place the koftas in a large bowl and pour warm gravy over them. Serve immediately with roti or naan.

Rice & Biryanis

CHICKPEAS PULAO

 PREPTIME **5 MINS** | COOKTIME **15 MINS** | GF VE

Quick and easy one-pot rice dish which can be prepared by cooking rice with chickpeas and few aromatic whole spices. Chickpeas not only enhance the taste but also add lot of nutrients and protein to this dish making it wholesome and satiating. Chickpeas or Chana Pulao is one of those versatile rice dishes that tastes divine on its own but also goes well with any curry. It can also be served with yogurt or vegetable raita. No wonder it is one of the most popular side-dishes that people choose to learn in my one-to-one online cooking classes.

Ingredients:

1 cup basmati rice

1 tin (400g) boiled chickpeas

1 medium-sized red onion, thinly sliced

2 tablespoons oil

1 teaspoon cumin seeds

1 cinnamon stick

1 black cardamom

2 bay leaves

2 cloves

½ teaspoon red chilli powder or to taste (optional)

Salt to taste

Makes: 2-3 servings

Method:

Soak the rice in enough water for 15-20 minutes.

Heat oil in a large non-stick pan. Add cumin seeds, cinnamon, black cardamom, bay leaves and cloves. Sauté for a few seconds; be careful not to burn the whole spices.

Add the sliced onions and sauté till they turn golden brown.

Drain the tinned chickpeas and rinse them. Add the rinsed chickpeas, salt and red chilli powder (if using) to the pan. Mix well.

Add 2 cups of water and let it come to a sharp boil. When the water starts boiling, add the soaked rice (after draining the water) and cover the pan. Reduce the heat to lowest possible setting. Let the rice cook on low heat for 15 minutes.

Switch off the heat after 15 minutes but do not open the lid for another 15 minutes.

Fluff the rice gently using a fork.

Serve hot with yogurt or your choice of curry.

Recipe Tips:

The taste of the pulao depends upon the quality of rice used. I recommend using good quality long-grain basmati rice for a great tasting and flavourful pulao. If you can't find long-grain basmati rice, a good quality regular basmati rice would also work well.

I prefer using red onion as it imparts a deeper colour and flavour to the pulao after being caramelized. However, if it's not available; you can replace it with white onion.

It's really important to soak the rice before making this pulao. Soaking the rice will result in longer rice grains and fluffier pulao.

VEGETABLE PULAO

 **10 MINS** | **15 MINS** | **GF** **V**

Flavourful one-pot rice dish that can be put together in few minutes. It's my go-to meal for the days when I am super-tired or not in a mood to cook an elaborate meal. It tastes great on its own but can be paired with a refreshing raita or any curry of your choice.

Ingredients:

1 cup basmati rice

½ cup peas

½ cup grated carrots

¼ cup sweet corn

1 red onion (sliced)

2 tablespoons oil

1 tablespoon ghee (can be replaced with oil)

1 teaspoon cumin seeds

1 cinnamon stick

2 bay leaves

1 black cardamom

2 cloves

½ teaspoon red chilli powder or to taste

Salt to taste

Makes: 2-3 servings

Method:

Rinse and soak the rice in water for 15 minutes.

Heat 2 tablespoons oil and 1 tablespoon ghee in a large pan. Add the cumin seeds, black cardamom, cloves, cinnamon, bay leaves and sliced onions. Sauté till the onions turn golden brown in colour.

Add the peas, sweet corn, grated carrots, salt and red chilli powder (if using). Mix well. Add 2 cups of water and let it come to a sharp boil.

Drain the soaked rice and add it to the boiling water. Let it come to a boil again. Cover the pan and reduce the heat to the lowest possible setting. Let the rice cook on low heat for 15 minutes.

Switch off the heat after 15 minutes but do not uncover the rice for another 15 minutes.

After letting it rest for 15 minutes, fluff the rice gently with a fork or flat spatula.

Serve hot with raita or curry of your choice.

Recipe Tips:

Basmati rice works best for a fluffy and fragrant pulao. The cooking time and the quantity of water mentioned above is tried and tested on basmati rice.

It is important to use a large broad pan with lid to ensure that the rice stays fluffy. The rice may turn mushy if cooked in a deep vessel which is not very broad.

Make it Vegan

Replace ghee with cooking oil.

MASALA KHICHDI

 **10 MINS** |  **12-20 MINS** |

Masala Khichdi is a simple dish prepared by cooking rice with lentils, vegetables and spices. It is a super-easy one-pot dish that makes a wholesome meal by itself but tastes divine when topped with some ghee and accompanied with papad (poppadums), pickle & yogurt.

Ingredients:

1 cup basmati rice
¾ cup yellow mung dal
1 medium-sized potato, chopped
2 carrots, finely chopped or grated
½ cup peas
2 tablespoons ghee
1 teaspoon cumin seeds
¼ teaspoon asafoetida
1 stick of cinnamon
2-3 cloves
4-5 cloves of garlic, crushed
1 teaspoon freshly ground ginger
2 green chillies, finely chopped (optional)
1 teaspoon turmeric powder
1 teaspoon coriander powder
½ teaspoon amchur powder
½ teaspoon red chilli powder or to taste
Salt to taste

Makes: 4 servings

Make it Vegan

Replace ghee with cooking oil.

Method:

Wash the rice and mung dal together and soak it for 30 minutes.

Choose any one of the methods given below to prepare the Masala Khichdi.

Pressure Cooker Method

Heat ghee in a pressure cooker. Add cumin seeds, cinnamon stick, cloves and asafoetida. Sauté for a few seconds.

Add the carrots, potatoes, peas, garlic, ginger and green chillies. Add the salt, turmeric powder, coriander powder, amchur powder and red chilli powder. Cook on medium heat for a minute.

Drain the soaked rice and mung dal. Add it to the pressure cooker.

Add 3.5 cups of water. Mix well and cover with the pressure cooker lid. Pressure cook on high for 3 whistles and then reduce the heat to low. Cook on low heat for 3-4 minutes. Let the steam escape before opening the lid of the pressure cooker.

Pan Method

Heat ghee in a broad pan. Add cumin seeds, cinnamon stick, cloves and asafoetida. Sauté for a few seconds.

Add the carrots, potatoes, peas, garlic, ginger and green chillies. Add the salt, turmeric powder, coriander powder, amchur powder and red chilli powder. Cook on medium heat for a minute.

Drain the soaked rice and mung dal. Add it to the pan.

Add 3.5 cups of water and mix well. Let it come to a sharp boil. Cover the pan with a lid and cook on high heat for 1 minute. After 1 minute, reduce the heat to the lowest possible setting and let it cook for 20 minutes. Do not uncover the pan before 20 minutes.

Instant Pot Method

Switch on the Instant Pot and press the 'Saute' button. Heat ghee in the inner pot. Add cumin seeds, cinnamon stick, cloves and asafoetida. Sauté for a few seconds.

Add the carrots, potatoes, peas, garlic, ginger and green chillies. Add the salt, turmeric powder, coriander powder, amchur powder and red chilli powder. Saute for a minute.

Drain the soaked rice and mung dal. Add them to the pot.

Add 3.5 cups of water. Mix well and close the pot. Press the manual or pressure cook button and cook on high pressure for 12 minutes.

Let the pressure release naturally.

Serving the Khichdi

Serve hot with pickle, yogurt and papad (poppadum).

Recipe Tips:

You can use **any vegetables** of your choice.

You can **skip the green chillies** if you do not like spicy.

Please note that asafoetida is **naturally gluten-free** but some manufacturers sell it mixed with wheat flour. Please **check the ingredients** carefully if you are following a gluten-free diet.

> "
>
> The food was authentic, previously I tried few times looking on YouTube but I wasn't satisfied. This time I was very pleased. My kids loved the food. Thanks Tanu!
>
> *Sree S.*
>
>

LAMB YAKHNI PULAO

 **5 MINS** | **45 MINS** | **GF**

Lamb Yakhni Pulao is prepared by cooking rice & lamb in a flavourful lamb stock (called Yakhni) along with onions and whole spices. I also like to add potatoes in this pulao. It is one of the easiest lamb dishes and makes a complete meal.

Ingredients:

1.5 cups basmati rice

500g diced lamb (on-the-bone)

1 large red onion (sliced)

1 medium-sized potato, thinly sliced

2 tablespoons oil

1 tablespoon ghee

1 teaspoon cumin seeds

1 cinnamon stick

4 bay leaves

1 black cardamom

4 cloves

1 teaspoon coriander powder

½ teaspoon amchur powder (dried raw mango powder)

½ teaspoon red chilli powder (optional)

Salt to taste

Makes: 4 servings

Method:

Soaking the Rice

Rinse the rice and soak it in water for 15 minutes.

Cooking the Lamb

Choose any one of the methods given below to cook the lamb.

Pressure Cooker Method

Add the diced lamb, 1 cinnamon stick, 2 cloves, 1 black cardamom, 2 bay leaves, 1 teaspoon salt (or to taste) and 3 cups of water in a pressure cooker. Pressure cook on high for 4 whistles and then on low for 10 minutes. Let the pressure release naturally before opening the lid of the pressure cooker.

Instant Pot Method

Add the diced lamb, 1 cinnamon stick, 2 cloves, 1 black cardamom, 2 bay leaves, 1 teaspoon salt (or to taste) and 3 cups of water in an instant pot. Pressure cook on high pressure for 25 minutes with natural pressure release.

Pot Method

Add the diced lamb, 1 cinnamon stick, 2 cloves, 1 black cardamom, 2 bay leaves, 1 teaspoon salt (or to taste) and 3 cups of water in a pot. Let it come to a sharp boil and cover with a lid. Cook on medium heat for 45-60 minutes or till the lamb is cooked.

Preparing the Pulao

Heat 2 tablespoons oil along with 1 tablespoon ghee in a large pan. Add the cumin seeds, 2 cloves, 2 bay leaves, sliced onions and potatoes. Sauté till the onions turn golden brown in colour.

Gently remove the lamb pieces from the stock using a slotted ladle and add them to the pan. Add salt, coriander powder, amchur powder and red chilli powder. Sauté the lamb for 2-3 minutes stirring very gently to avoid breaking the lamb pieces.

Add 3 cups of lamb stock (water in which the lamb was boiled) and let it come to a sharp boil.

Drain the soaked rice and add it to the boiling stock. Let it come to a boil again. Cover the pan and reduce the heat to the lowest possible setting. Let the rice cook on low heat for 15 minutes.

Switch off the heat after 15 minutes but do not uncover the rice for another 15 minutes.

After letting it rest for 15 minutes, fluff the rice gently with a fork or flat spatula.

Serve hot with yogurt or cucumber raita (page 123).

Recipe Tips:

I highly recommend using on-the-bone lamb for this pulao. The juices from the bones add a great taste and flavour to the stock (yakhni) in which the rice is cooked. Meat form the lower leg of the lamb or the shoulder tastes best in this recipe.

People who tried this recipe:

Pulao is really yummy...
I will cook it again soon..

Amy

> The Lamb Pulao is out of the
> world...the meat is so tender,
> juicy and flavourful.
> Thanks for this amazing recipe.

James

POTATO & PEAS TEHRI

 **PREP**TIME **10 MINS** | **COOK**TIME **15 MINS** | **GF** **V**

Vegetable Tehri is quick and easy one-pot rice dish. It's a simple yet super-comforting dish that makes a wholesome meal on its own. This recipe uses potato & peas but you can add any veggies based on availability or your choice.

Ingredients:

1 cup basmati rice

1 medium-sized potato, peeled and cut into small pieces

½ cup green peas (fresh or frozen)

1 medium-sized onion, chopped

1 teaspoon ginger, finely chopped

2-3 green chillies, chopped (optional)

2 tablespoons ghee

2 teaspoons cumin seeds

¼ teaspoon asafoetida

2 cloves

1 small cinnamon stick (1 inch approximately)

2 bay leaves

1 teaspoon turmeric powder

1 teaspoon coriander powder

Salt to taste

Makes: 2-3 servings

Make it Vegan
Replace ghee with cooking oil.

Method:

Wash the rice and soak it for 15 minutes.

Heat ghee in a broad pan or pot, add cumin seeds and allow them to splutter. Add asafoetida, cloves, bay leaves and cinnamon stick. Sauté for 5 seconds.

Add the chopped onions and potatoes. Sauté for 2-3 minutes or till the onions turn light golden brown in colour.

Add the peas, ginger, green chillies, salt, turmeric powder and coriander powder. Mix well and sauté for 30 seconds.

Add 2 cups of water and let it come to a sharp boil.

Drain the soaked rice and add them. Mix gently.

Cover the pot and cook on high heat for 1 minute. After 1 minute, reduce the heat to the lowest possible setting and let it cook for 15 minutes. Please do not uncover the pot before 15 minutes as it will let the steam to escape and the rice will not be cooked properly.

Turn off the heat after 15 minutes and let the rice rest for 5 minutes.

After letting it rest for 5 minutes, fluff the rice gently with a fork or spatula.

Serve hot with pickle.

Recipe Tips:

Do not skimp on the ghee as it imparts a very distinct flavour to this dish making it heavenly delicious. However, if you follow a vegan diet; you can replace the **ghee** with any cooking oil of your choice.

It is important to use a **large broad pan** with lid to ensure that the rice stays fluffy. The rice may turn mushy if cooked in a deep vessel which is not very broad.

Please note that asafoetida is **naturally gluten-free** but some manufacturers sell it mixed with wheat flour. Please **check the ingredients** carefully if you are following a gluten-free diet.

CHICKEN DUM BIRYANI

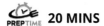 **20 MINS** | **Marination Time : 6-8 HRS** | **25 MINS** |

An aromatic and delectable rice dish in which layers of marinated chicken and rice are cooked using a special technique called **Dum**. The Dum technique involves slow cooking food in a pan/pot sealed with dough or foil to prevent the steam from escaping. The process locks the delicate flavour of the spices and herbs enabling the dish to thoroughly absorb these flavours. Chicken Dum Biryani tastes divine on its own but a bowl of raita on the side makes a great combination.

Ingredients:

For marinating
750g baby chicken cut into small pieces
2 tablespoons biryani masala
1 teaspoon red chilli powder (optional)
¾ cup whisked yogurt
2 tablespoons fresh garlic paste
1 tablespoon fresh ginger paste
1 tablespoon lemon juice
Salt to taste

For boiling the rice
1 cup + ¼ cup Basmati Rice
1 cinnamon stick
4 cloves
1 star anise
2 bay leaves
1 black cardamom
1 teaspoon ghee
Salt to taste

For the layering
1 cup finely chopped coriander leaves
8-10 mint leaves, finely chopped
A few strands of saffron (about a pinch)
1 teaspoon kewra water
2 teaspoons biryani masala
1 tablespoon ghee

Other Ingredients
2 large onions, thinly sliced
4 tablespoons oil

Makes: 4 servings

Method:

Marinating the chicken

Combine the chicken and all the ingredients for marinating in a large bowl. Mix well and cover with a cling film. Keep in the refrigerator. The biryani tastes best if the chicken is marinated for 6-8 hours or overnight. If you do not have that much time, marinate the chicken for as much time as you can and at least for an hour.

Boiling the Rice

Wash the rice and soak them for 15-20 minutes. Drain & keep aside. Boil 5 cups of water in a large pan. Add the rice, cloves, cinnamon stick, star anise, bay leaves, black cardamom, ghee and salt. Let it come to a sharp boil. Cover the pan and reduce the heat to lowest possible setting. Boil the rice for 7-8 minutes. After 8 minutes, drain the rice using a colander. Rinse the rice with cold water. Drain thoroughly and keep aside.

Preparation for Layering

Take 1 teaspoon kewra water and 2 tablespoons water in a bowl. Microwave it for 10 seconds just to make it lukewarm. Add the saffron strands to it and cover it. Keep aside.

Heat oil in a pan and fry the sliced onions till golden brown. Place them on a dish lined with kitchen towel. Keep aside.

Cooking the Chicken

In the same oil, add the marinated chicken and cook on high heat for 3-4 minutes. Add half of the fried onions. Cover the pan and cook on medium heat for about 7 minutes or till the chicken gets nicely cooked. Remove & keep aside.

Layering

Take a large pan (preferably broad and not too deep). Grease it with ghee. Spread about one-third of the cooked rice on the base. Sprinkle the coriander leaves, mint leaves, fried onions, a pinch of biryani masala and 1 teaspoon of ghee. Drizzle half of the kewra-saffron water. Then add almost ½ of the cooked chicken. Repeat the same process by adding one more layer of rice and chicken. Add rice on the top layer to cover the chicken.

Slow-Cooking

Cover the pan with aluminium foil first and then with a lid so that no steam escapes.

Place this pan on a pre-heated flat pan, reduce the heat to lowest possible setting and cook for 15-20 minutes. If your biryani pan has a thick base, you don't need to put the flat pan under it.

After cooking for 15-20 minutes, turn off the heat but **do not uncover the pan** for another 15 minutes.

Mix gently with a fork or spatula without breaking the rice. Avoid over mixing.

Serving the Biryani

Serve warm with raita. It also tastes great on its own.

Recipe Tips:

Biryani Masala is available in the Asian section of supermarkets or Indian supermarkets. However, if you wish to make your own biryani masala; please check the recipe in the **Spice-Mixes Section** (page 13) of the book.

The taste of the biryani depends upon the quality of rice in addition to the cooking method. Please use the best quality basmati rice that you can get your hands on and try to use extra-long basmati rice if possible.

Please use a large broad pan to ensure that the rice stays fluffy. The rice may turn mushy if cooked in a deep vessel which is not very broad.

People who tried this recipe:

That was brilliant!
We finished all of it.

Satwinder

I attended Tanu's cooking classes and I learned how to make excellent Biryani. My husband loves Biryani and I always wanted to learn how to do it. I didn't know that in just one class I can master it. It turned out heavenly delicious.

Karolina Belzyt

The Biryani we made yesterday turned out to be awesome ..much superior than the fine dining restaurant we dine in :)

Ranjani & Srini

PANEER DUM BIRYANI

 **20 MINS** | **25 MINS** | **GF** **V**

A delectable rice dish made by slow cooking curried paneer between layers of rice. If you are a vegetarian or a paneer lover; it's a must-try dish for you.

Ingredients:

For boiling the rice
1 cup Basmati Rice
4 cloves
1 cinnamon stick
    (Approximately 1 inch)
1 star anise
2 bay leaves
1 black cardamom
1 teaspoon ghee
Salt to taste

Other Ingredients
250g Paneer, cubed
2 large onions, thinly sliced
2 tomatoes (pureed)
1 tablespoon garlic paste
1 tablespoon ginger paste
3-4 tablespoons oil
1 tablespoon ghee
½ cup finely chopped
    coriander leaves
8-10 mint leaves, finely
    chopped
A few strands of saffron
    (about a pinch)
1 teaspoon kewra water
2 tablespoons Biryani Masala
1 teaspoon coriander powder
1 teaspoon red chilli powder
    (optional)
Salt to taste

Makes: 4 servings

Method:

Boiling the Rice

Wash the rice and soak them for 15-20 minutes. Drain & keep aside. Boil 5 cups of water in a large saucepan. Add the rice, cloves, cinnamon stick, star anise, bay leaves, black cardamom, ghee and salt. Cover the saucepan and reduce the heat to low. Boil the rice for 8 minutes. After 8 minutes, drain the rice using a colander. Rinse the rice with cold water. Drain thoroughly and keep aside.

Preparation for Layering

Mix 2 tablespoons water with 1 teaspoon kewra water in a small bowl. Add the saffron strands to it and keep aside.

Heat oil in a pan and fry half of the sliced onions till golden brown. Place them on a dish lined with kitchen towel. Keep aside.

In the same oil, add the remaining onions along with the ginger & garlic paste. Sauté till they turn golden brown. Add the tomato puree, salt, coriander powder, red chilli powder (if using) and biryani masala. Sauté till oil starts oozing.

Add a tablespoon of oil in a separate flat non-stick pan. Place the paneer cubes and pan-fry on each side till light golden-brown.

Add the pan-fried paneer to the prepared onion-tomato masala and mix well. Cover the pan and cook for a minute so that the paneer absorbs the flavours of the spices.

Layering the Rice & Paneer

Take a large pan. Grease it with ghee. Spread about half of the cooked rice on the base. Sprinkle the coriander leaves, mint leaves, fried onions, a pinch of biryani masala and 1 teaspoon of ghee. Layer the prepared onion-tomato masala with paneer on top of the rice. Add the remaining rice on the top to cover the paneer layer. Sprinkle some coriander leaves and fried onions on the top. Sprinkle the saffron infused kewra water on the rice using a teaspoon.

Slow Cooking

Cover the pan with aluminium foil first and then with a lid so that no steam escapes.

Place this pan on a pre-heated flat pan, reduce the heat to lowest possible setting and cook for 15-20 minutes. If your biryani pan has a thick base, you don't need to put the flat pan under it.

After cooking for 15-20 minutes, turn off the heat but **do not uncover the pan** for another 15 minutes.

Mix gently with a spatula without breaking the rice. Do not overmix.

Serve with raita of your choice.

Recipe Tips:

Biryani Masala is available in the Asian section of supermarkets or Indian supermarkets. However, if you wish to make your own biryani masala; please check the recipe in the **Spice-Mixes Section** (page 13) of the book.

Be careful not to overcook the paneer while pan-frying it. Just remove it as soon as it gets a very light golden colour. Over-cooking the paneer can make it hard and chewy.

Please use a large broad pan to ensure that the rice stays fluffy. The rice may turn mushy if cooked in a deep vessel which is not very broad.

VEGETABLE DUM BIRYANI

 **20 MINS** | **35 MINS** |

Vegetable Biryani is an unsung rice dish since it is overshadowed by the meat varieties. It is prepared by slow-cooking curried vegetables between layers of rice. The delicate combination of spices and herbs along with the unique cooking technique makes this dish a real treat for your taste buds.

Ingredients:

For boiling the rice
1 cup Basmati Rice
4 cloves
1 cinnamon stick (approximately 1 inch)
1 star anise
2 bay leaves
1 black cardamom
1 teaspoon ghee
Salt to taste

Other Ingredients
1 large potato thinly sliced
1-2 carrots cut into thin sticks
1 cup cauliflower cut into small florets
Fine green beans cut into 1 inch pieces
2 large onions, thinly sliced
1 tomato, sliced
1 tablespoon garlic paste
1 tablespoon ginger paste
1/3 cup whisked yogurt
3-4 tablespoons oil
1 tablespoon ghee
½ cup finely chopped coriander leaves
8-10 mint leaves, finely chopped
A few strands of saffron (about a pinch)
1 teaspoon kewra water
2 tablespoons Biryani Masala
1 teaspoon red chilli powder (optional)
Salt to taste

Makes: 4 servings

Method:

Boiling the Rice

Wash the rice and soak them for 15-20 minutes. Drain & keep aside. Boil 5 cups of water in a large saucepan. Add the rice, cloves, cinnamon stick, star anise, bay leaves, black cardamom, ghee and salt. Cover the saucepan and reduce the heat to low. Boil the rice for 8 minutes. After 8 minutes, drain the rice using a colander. Rinse the rice with cold water. Drain thoroughly and keep aside.

Preparation for Layering

Mix 2 tablespoons water with 1 teaspoon kewra water in a small bowl. Add the saffron strands to it and keep aside.

Heat oil in a pan and fry the sliced onions till golden brown. Place them on a dish lined with kitchen towel. Keep aside.

In the same oil, add the sliced potatoes and sauté them till they become golden brown on the edges and get almost cooked (about 90%). Take them out in a large bowl. Repeat the same process with the remaining vegetables sautéing them separately and taking them out in the same bowl.

Add the ginger & garlic paste to the same pan and sauté till light golden brown. Add half of the fried onions and the whisked yogurt. Keep stirring continuously till the oil starts separating from the masala. Add all the vegetables, salt, biryani masala and red chilli powder (if using). Mix well and sauté for a minute. Keep aside.

Layering the Rice & Vegetables:

Take a large broad pan. Grease it with ghee and place the tomato slices at the bottom. Spread about one-third of the cooked rice on top of the tomato slices. Sprinkle the coriander leaves, mint leaves, fried onions, a pinch of biryani masala and 1 teaspoon of ghee. Put a layer of prepared vegetables. Repeat the same process by adding one more layer of rice and vegetables. Add rice on the top layer to cover the vegetables.

Sprinkle some coriander leaves, mint leaves, fried onions and a pinch of biryani masala on the top. Sprinkle the saffron infused kewra water on the rice using a teaspoon.

Cover the pan with aluminium foil first and then with a lid so that no steam escapes.

Place this pan on a pre-heated flat pan, reduce the heat to the lowest possible setting and cook for 15-20 minutes. If your biryani pan has a thick base, you don't need to put the flat pan under it.

After cooking for 15-20 minutes, turn off the heat but **do not uncover the pan** for another 15 minutes.

Mix gently with a spatula without breaking the rice. Do not overmix.

Serve with raita of your choice.

Recipe Tips:

Biryani Masala is available in the Asian section of supermarkets or Indian supermarkets. However, if you wish to make your own biryani masala; please check the recipe in the **Spice-Mixes Section** (page 13) of the book.

The taste of the biryani depends upon the quality of rice in addition to the cooking method. Please use the best quality basmati rice that you can get your hands on and try to use extra-long basmati rice if possible.

Please use a large broad pan to ensure that the rice stays fluffy. The rice may turn mushy if cooked in a deep vessel which is not very broad.

Snacks & Starters

BAKED SAMOSA

 **30 MINS** | **25 MINS** | **V**

Samosa is an all-time favourite deep-fried Indian snack and a popular street food in India. This is a quick and guilt-free version of samosa which can be easily prepared at home. These flaky, crispy and super-delicious samosas are prepared using ready rolled puff pastry sheet and a delicious potatoes & peas filling. They freeze well and you can put them straight in the oven from the freezer; they don't need to be thawed.

Ingredients:

1 ready rolled puff pastry sheet

3-4 boiled potatoes (peeled and roughly broken into pieces)

½ cup peas

½ teaspoon cumin seeds

¼ teaspoon asafoetida

½ teaspoon coriander powder

½ teaspoon turmeric powder

½ teaspoon red chilli powder or to taste

1 teaspoon amchur powder (dried mango powder)

2 tablespoons oil

Salt to taste

Makes: 8

Make it Gluten-Free

Use gluten free ready rolled puff pastry sheets.

Make sure the asafoetida you are using has no wheat flour mixed in it or you can simply skip it.

Method:

Preheat the oven to 180°C .

Heat oil in a large pan and add the cumin seeds. Let them crackle and add the asafoetida. Then add the peas, a pinch of salt and a splash of water. Cover the pan and reduce the heat to low. Let the peas cook for 2-3 minutes.

Add the boiled potatoes, salt, turmeric powder, coriander powder, amchur and red chilli powder. Mix well, cover the pan and reduce the heat to low. Let them cook on low heat for 2 minutes.

After 2 minutes, uncover the pan and mix well. Take the potatoes out in a large dish and let them cool.

Take the ready rolled puff pastry sheet out of the fridge. Open it into a flat sheet and lay it on the worktop along with the baking paper it is wrapped in.

Cut it into 8 equal sized squares using a pizza cutter or a knife.

Add a tablespoon or more of potato filling on each square, fold it into a rectangle or triangle pressing the edges together with your fingers.

Place them on a large baking tray along with the baking paper.

Bake in the preheated oven for 20-25 minutes at 180 degrees Celsius. Serve warm.

Recipe Tips:

Keep the puff pastry sheet chilled at all times. Take it out of the refrigerator only when you have prepared the filling and you are ready to make the samosas. If you notice that it is getting sticky or not easy to handle, put it in the freezer for 10-15 minutes.

These samosas taste best when they are warm and crispy. They should be consumed within **1-2 hours of baking** after which they won't stay that crisp.

To freeze the samosas; just place them flat in a tray after stuffing them with the filling. Cover with cling film place the tray in the freezer for 6-8 hours. After that, you can put them in a freezer bag and store in the freezer. Whenever you want to eat them, bake in a pre-heated oven directly from the freezer. No need to thaw them. The frozen ones will take extra baking time of 5-10 minutes.

ONION BHAJIYA

 **PREP**TIME **15 MINS** | **COOK**TIME **20 MINS** | GF VE

One of the most popular Indian snacks made with onions, gram flour, spices and herbs. It is also known as Onion Pakora or Kanda Bhaji. It tastes best when served hot with green chutney and tea.

Ingredients:

2 large onions, thinly sliced

1 teaspoon freshly ground garlic (optional)

½ teaspoon freshly ground ginger

½ cup finely chopped fresh coriander leaves (optional)

½ cup besan (chickpea flour/ gram flour)

½ teaspoon carom seeds

½ teaspoon coriander powder

¼ teaspoon baking soda

½ teaspoon chaat masala

½ teaspoon red chilli powder or to taste

½ teaspoon amchur powder

Salt to taste

Oil for deep-frying

Makes: 4 servings

Method:

Preparing the batter

Combine all the ingredients for bhajiyas (except oil and chaat masala) in a large bowl. Mix well. Add about ¼ cup of water or as required to make a thick batter. We do not want a runny batter. When you drop a spoonful of batter, it should fall in lumps. Let the batter rest for 20 minutes.

Onion bhajiya can be deep-fried or air-fried. Choose any one of the methods given below.

Deep-Frying Method

Heat oil in a pan for deep-frying. The oil should be medium hot to fry perfect bhajiyas. To check if the oil is medium hot, drop a bit of batter into the oil; the batter should come up but not change colour right away.

Drop 6-8 spoonfuls (depending on the size of your pan) of the bhajiya mixture into the oil. Deep fry the bhajiyas on medium heat till they turn golden brown and crispy from all sides. Place them on a dish lined with kitchen towel/ absorbent paper napkins to get rid of the excess oil.

Repeat the same process for rest of the bhajiya mixture.

Air-Fryer Method

Preheat the air-fryer at 190 degrees Celsius for 10 minutes. Line the air-fryer basket with aluminium foil or baking paper and grease it with spray oil. Using a cookie scoop, place scoops of batter on it, leaving some space in between. You should be able to make 8-10 bhajiyas in one batch depending upon the size of your air-fryer basket. Spray some cooking oil over the bhajiyas. Air fry the bhajiyas at 190 degrees Celsius for 12 minutes.

After 12 minutes, turn them over and spray some cooking oil over the bhajiyas. Air-fry for another 3-5 minutes or till they turn golden brown and crispy.

Serving the Bhajiyas

Sprinke some chaat masala on the bhajiyas and serve hot with tomato ketchup, green chutney (page 125) or mango chutney (page 127).

TANDOORI VEGETARIAN PLATTER

 **20 MINS** | **Marination Time : 30 MINS** **15 MINS** |

Tandoori Platter is a breeze to prepare and it's super versatile. It can be served as a starter and makes a wholesome meal if paired with rice or naan.

Ingredients:

For marinating paneer & veggies
½ cup Greek yogurt
1.5 tablespoons roasted gram flour (besan)
1 tablespoon oil
4-5 cloves of garlic, freshly ground
½ teaspoon freshly ground ginger
1 tablespoon lemon juice or to taste
1 tablespoon Kashmiri red chilli powder
½ teaspoon red chilli powder (optional)
¼ teaspoon garam masala
1 teaspoon chaat masala
1 teaspoon kasuri methi
Salt to taste

For marinating pineapple
100g pineapple cut into cubes
1 teaspoon lemon juice
1 teaspoon honey
½ teaspoon black salt
½ teaspoon chaat masala
A pinch of red chilli powder (optional)

Other Ingredients
300g Paneer cut into cubes
100g baby button mushrooms
1 small red onion (cut into chunks and layers separated)
½ red pepper (cut into squares)
2 tablespoons oil

Equipment
Wooden Skewers
Large Grill Pan or Flat Non-stick Pan

Makes: 3-4 servings

Method:

Take a large bowl. Mix together all the ingredients for marinating the paneer & vegetables.

Add the paneer cubes, mushrooms, onions and red peppers. Mix well so that they get well coated with the marinade. Leave aside for 15-30 minutes.

Take a large bowl. Mix together all the ingredients for marinating the pineapple. Keep aside.

Skewer the marinated paneer, onions and peppers alternating between each.

Skewer the pineapple cubes and mushrooms separately as cooking times may vary.

Drizzle some oil on a flat non-stick pan or a grill pan and let it get heated.

Place the skewers on the pan and reduce the heat to medium. Keep rotating the skewers so that all the sides get evenly cooked.

Serve warm with a lemon wedge on the side.

Make it Vegan

Use extra-firm tofu instead of paneer. Press tofu with a heavy object for 15 minutes to drain the excess moisture.

Replace the regular yogurt with yogurt made from coconut milk.

KULLE CHAAT

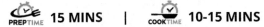 **PREP**TIME **15 MINS** | **COOK**TIME **10-15 MINS** |

A unique and healthy chaat in which bite-sized fruits and vegetables are stuffed with a delectable mix of chickpeas, pomegranate seeds, lemon juice and spices. It's a street-food speciality from Old Delhi. A combination of sweet, spicy and tangy flavours is surely going to please your taste-buds.

Ingredients:

1 large slice of watermelon cut into thick roundels using a cookie cutter

2 bananas

2 boiled potatoes

2 tomatoes

1 cucumber cut into cylinders (about 1 inch in height)

1 cup boiled chickpeas (tinned)

½ cup pomegranate arils

2 tablespoons lemon juice

1 tablespoon chaat masala or to taste

1 teaspoon roasted cumin powder

¼ teaspoon red chilli powder (optional)

½ teaspoon black salt

Salt to taste

Makes: 2-3 servings

Method:

Preparing the Stuffing

Combine the boiled chickpeas, pomegranate seeds, 1 tablespoon lemon juice, 1.5 teaspoons chaat masala, ¼ teaspoon red chilli powder (if using), 1 teaspoon roasted cumin powder and salt in a large bowl. Mix well and keep aside.

Preparing the Fruits & Vegetables

Cut the tomatoes and boiled potatoes into 2 halves.

Peel the bananas and cut them horizontally into 2 halves. Make a vertical slit in the banana halves.

Cut the watermelon slice into thick roundels using a cookie-cutter or a sharp-edged small bowl.

Cut the cucumber into cylinders (about 1 inch height).

Scoop out the centre from all the prepared fruits and vegetables (except bananas) using a small cookie scoop or a sharp-edged spoon.

Assembling & Serving

Place the prepared fruits & vegetables on a large serving platter or individual serving plates.

Squeeze them generously with lemon juice. Sprinkle black salt and chaat masala.

Fill them with the prepared stuffing and serve immediately.

Recipe Tips:

You can use any seasonal **fruits or vegetables of your choice**. Some other options are papaya, guava, apple and boiled sweet potatoes.

To boil the potatoes, add 2 medium-sized potatoes along with 2 cups of water in a **pressure cooker**. Pressure cook on high for 4-5 whistles. Let the steam escape before opening the lid of pressure cooker. They can also be boiled in an **instant pot** for 10 minutes on high pressure with natural pressure release. You can also boil them in a **saucepan** until done.

PEANUTS BHAJIYA

 **10 MINS** | **20 MINS** | GF VE

Crunchy peanuts coated with gram flour and spices. This recipe prepares a guilt-free & healthier version by baking them instead of deep-frying. Peanut bhajiya is a popular Indian snack enjoyed with tea. It also makes a great starter or an accompaniment with drinks if mixed with finely chopped onions and freshly squeezed lemon juice.

Ingredients:

1 cup raw peanuts

5 tablespoons gram flour (besan)

2 tablespoons poha (rice flakes)

1 tablespoon water

2 tablespoons oil

½ teaspoon black salt

½ teaspoon + 1 teaspoon chaat masala

½ teaspoon + ½ teaspoon red chilli powder(optional)

½ teaspoon turmeric powder

Salt to taste

Makes: 3-4 servings

Method:

Add the poha (rice flakes) in a spice grinder and coarsely grind it. Do not grind it into a fine powder. Keep aside.

Combine gram flour, coarsely ground poha, black salt, chaat masala (½ teaspoon), red chilli powder (½ teaspoon), turmeric powder and salt in a bowl. Mix well.

Take the peanuts in a large sieve and rinse them under running water while shaking the sieve a few times so that all the peanuts get rinsed properly. The idea is to make them wet so that they get nicely coated with the flour and spice mixture.

Add these peanuts in the bowl containing flour and spice mixture. Mix well so that all the peanuts get nicely coated with this mixture. Drizzle some oil (about 1 tablespoon) over the peanuts and mix well. Add about a teaspoon of water and mix well. At this stage, all the flour should get coated on the peanuts.

Preheat the oven to 180C and line a baking tray with baking paper. Drizzle some oil (about ½ tablespoon) on the baking paper and spread it with a brush to grease it properly. You can also use spray oil for this step.

Place the peanuts on the greased baking tray in a single layer and bake in the pre-heated oven at 180C for 18 minutes. (Take the baking tray out after 9 minutes, shake it gently and spray some oil. Place it back in the oven for another 9 minutes).

Sprinkle some chaat masala (about 1 teaspoon or to taste) and red chilli powder (½ teaspoon if using) as soon as you take them out of the oven. Shake the tray so that the peanuts get coated with the masala.

Let them cool completely and transfer in an air-right container. They stay good for up to 4 weeks.

CHICKEN TIKKA

 15 MINS | **Marination Time : 6-8 HRS** | **10 MINS** |

Chicken tikka needs no introduction. These succulent chunks of marinated chicken make a great starter and a delicious meal when served with naan or rice along with some refreshing salad.

Ingredients:

300g diced chicken breast

2 tablespoons Greek yogurt

1 teaspoon freshly ground garlic

½ teaspoon freshly ground ginger

1 small onion (cut into chunks and layers separated)

½ red pepper (cut into squares)

1 tablespoon + 2 tablespoons oil

1 tablespoon lemon juice

2 teaspoons Kashmiri red chilli powder

½ teaspoon garam masala

1 teaspoon coriander powder

½ teaspoon cumin powder

Salt to taste

Makes: 2-3 servings

Method:

Combine the chicken pieces, onions and red peppers with rest of the ingredients in a large bowl. Add 1 tablespoon oil and mix well.

Cover the bowl and keep in the refrigerator overnight or for 6-8 hours for best results.

Skewer the marinated chicken pieces, onions and peppers alternating between each.

Drizzle some oil in a grill or flat pan and heat it. Once heated, place the skewers on the pan and keep the heat to medium-high. Cook for 2-3 minutes, drizzle some oil on the chicken tikka and rotate the skewers. Keep rotating the skewers after intervals of 2 minutes till the chicken is evenly cooked from all sides.

Serve warm with a lemon wedge on the side.

Recipe Tips:

Be careful **not to overcook** the chicken otherwise it can turn rubbery. Chicken breast cooks very fast; it should take 5-7 minutes. To check if it is cooked through, cut one of the biggest pieces in the middle with a knife- it should be all white from inside when cooked thoroughly. If it looks light pink from inside, it's not done yet.

If you are **unable to marinate** the chicken for 6-8 hours, you can prepare it by marinating for 1 hour but the taste will not be the same.

Chicken Tikka tastes best when eaten **warm and fresh** from the grill. The marinated chicken can be kept in the refrigerator for up to 2 days. Prepare the salad, dip or the sides you are going to serve it with and grill it when you are ready to eat it.

HARA BHARA KEBAB

 **20 MINS** | **10 MINS** |

Delicious patties loaded with greens. They are usually deep-fried but I have used the pan-frying method in this recipe to make them healthier. When preparing for guests or a big batch; you might find it easier to deep-fry them. Whatever way you choose to prepare them, they simply taste divine.

Ingredients:

200g baby spinach

2 large potatoes, boiled

½ cup green peas

½ cup fresh coriander leaves

1.5 teaspoon freshly ground ginger

2 green chillies, crushed or finely chopped

1-2 bread slices

1 tablespoon corn flour

½ teaspoon roasted cumin powder (optional)

1 teaspoon chaat masala

½ teaspoon amchur powder (dried mango powder)

2-3 tablespoons oil

Salt to taste

Makes: 2-3 servings

Method:

Combine the washed spinach leaves and peas in a pan. Cook on medium heat for 2 minutes while stirring continuously. The spinach will get wilted and release water. Once the spinach releases water, cook on high heat for 2-3 minutes (while stirring frequently) or till all the moisture gets evaporated. Remove from the pan and keep aside to let it cool.

Once cooled, transfer it to a grinder. Add the coriander leaves, ginger and green chillies. Grind to a paste.

Mash the boiled potatoes in a large bowl. Add the green paste, salt, amchur powder, roasted cumin powder, chaat masala and corn flour. Mix well.

Take 2 bread slices and dip them in water. Squeeze them between your palms to get rid of all the water. Mash them and add them to the kebab mixture. Mix well.

Shape the mixture into round or oval kebabs.

Drizzle oil in a flat pan. Once hot, place the kebabs on the pan. Pan fry on medium-low heat for 2-3 minutes or till golden brown. Turn them over and pan-fry for another 2-3 minutes or till golden brown.

Serve warm on their own or wrapped in a paratha with salad & chutney.

Make it Gluten-Free

Use gluten-free bread slices.

CHANA CHAAT

 **15 MINS** |

Chana (chickpeas) Chaat is vibrant, tangy and healthy snack which can be put together in no time. It's almost a no-cook recipe if you are using tinned chickpeas. It can be eaten as a snack or served as an appetizer. It's also a great post-workout snack.

Ingredients:

400g tin of boiled chickpeas (drained & rinsed) or 1.5 cups boiled chickpeas

1-2 boiled potatoes, cut into small pieces

1 tablespoon lemon juice

1 tablespoon mint chutney (page 125)

1 tablespoon tamarind sauce/chutney

1 medium-sized onion, finely chopped

1 medium-sized tomato, finely chopped

1-2 teaspoon green chillies, finely chopped (optional)

1 tablespoon finely chopped coriander leaves

1 teaspoon chaat masala

½ teaspoon roasted cumin powder

¼ teaspoon red chilli powder (optional)

Salt to taste

Makes: 2-3 servings

Method:

Combine all the ingredients in a large bowl. Mix well.

Serve immediately garnished with coriander leaves.

Recipe Tips:

You can prepare it without the chutneys if you do not have them at hand. Just use the lemon juice and spices; it would taste like a **refreshing salad**. Feel free to add more veggies of your choice like cucumber, grated carrots etc.

To boil the chickpeas (if not using tinned chickpeas), soak 1 cup chickpeas overnight for 6-8 hours. Drain the water. Add them to a pressure cooker along with 2.5 cups of water and pressure cook on high heat for 6-7 whistles. Reduce the heat to low and pressure cook for 15 minutes. Let the steam escape before opening the lid of pressure cooker. Drain the chana by passing them through a sieve and collecting the water in a bowl. This water can be used in a soup or curry. They can also be boiled in an **Instant Pot** for 20-25 minutes on high pressure with natural pressure release.

To boil the potatoes, add 2 medium-sized potatoes along with 2 cups of water in a pressure cooker. Pressure cook on high for 4-5 whistles. Let the steam escape before opening the lid of pressure cooker. They can also be boiled in an **Instant Pot** for 10 minutes on high pressure with natural pressure release. You can also boil them in a **saucepan** until done.

Tamarind sauce/chutney can be bought from any Indian store or Asian section of most supermarkets.

CHICKEN PAKORA

 15 MINS | **Marinating Time: 20 MINS** | **20 MINS** |

Addictively delicious and succulent chicken morsels in a crispy and flavourful coating. They make a brilliant crowd-pleasing snack for the parties or get-togethers. They can also be wrapped in a tortilla along with some mint chutney (page 125) or mango chutney (page 127) to make a tasty meal.

Ingredients:

250g chicken breast (diced into bite-size pieces)

1 teaspoon freshly ground garlic (3 garlic cloves)

1 teaspoon freshly ground ginger

2 tablespoons finely chopped fresh coriander

1 egg white

1 tablespoon lemon juice

3 tablespoons gram flour

2 tablespoons poha (rice flakes)

¼ teaspoon turmeric powder

1.5 teaspoon Kashmiri red chilli powder or to taste

½ teaspoon chaat masala

Salt to taste

Oil for deep frying

Makes: 4 servings

Method:

Add the poha (rice flakes) in a spice grinder and coarsely grind it. Do not grind it into a fine powder. Keep aside.

Combine the chicken breast, freshly ground garlic & ginger, lemon juice, egg white, chopped coriander, salt, turmeric and red chilli powder in a large bowl. Mix well.

Mix the gram flour and the coarsely ground rice flakes in a separate bowl and add it to the chicken. Mix well.

If the batter is too thick, add 1-2 tablespoons of water and mix well. Keep it aside and let it rest for 20-30 minutes.

Heat the oil for deep frying. Drop in the chicken pieces one by one. Fry for 2 -3 minutes on medium heat. Add 5-6 chicken pieces at one time depending upon the size of the vessel used for deep-frying.

Turn over the chicken pieces and fry again for 2 -3 minutes on medium heat.

Take them out in a dish lined with kitchen towel. Sprinkle some chaat masala on them.

Enjoy warm with a dip of your choice.

Recipe Tips:

It's very important to fry these pakoras at the **right temperature**. They need to be fried in medium hot oil. If the oil is too hot, they will brown very quickly and can stay raw from inside. If the oil is not hot enough, they can become oily and rubbery due to longer cooking time.

The **size of the chicken pieces** should not be too big otherwise they can stay raw from within. Cut them approximately into 1-inch cubes.

Kashmiri Red Chilli Powder is not very hot; it will impart a bright colour to these pakoras without making them too spicy. If you would like to make **spicier pakoras**, you can use the regular red chilli powder or finely chopped green chillies.

ALOO TIKKI CHAAT

 **PREP**TIME **30 MINS** | **COOK**TIME **20 MINS** | **V**

Delicious potato patties (tikkis) topped with whisked yogurt, chutneys and spices. Each bite creates a burst of flavours in the mouth. It is one of the most-loved street foods in India.The tikkis are usually deep fried to make them crispy but you can also pan-fry them.

Ingredients:

Aloo Tikki

5 medium-sized potatoes (boiled, peeled & mashed)

½ cup boiled green peas

2-3 slices of brown/white bread

½ cup coarsely ground poha

1 teaspoon freshly ground ginger

2-3 finely chopped ground green chillies or to taste

2 tablespoons finely chopped coriander leaves

2 teaspoons chaat masala

1 teaspoon cumin seeds

Salt to taste

Oil for deep-frying

Serving

1 cup whisked yogurt

Mint chutney (page 123) to taste

Tamarind sauce/chutney to taste

1 teaspoon roasted cumin powder

1 teaspoon red chilli powder (optional)

1 teaspoon chaat masala

½ cup finely chopped onions

1-2 tablespoons fresh pomegranate seeds

Makes: 10-12 tikkis

Method:

In a large bowl, combine all the ingredients for aloo tikki except bread and oil. Dip the bread slices in water and squeeze them between your palms to get rid of the excess water. Mash them into the aloo tikki mixture and mix well.

Grease your palms with oil. Take a portion of aloo tikki mixture and shape it into a ball. Flatten it gently between your palms to give it the shape of a tikki. Repeat the same process to make tikkis from the remaining mixture.

Heat oil for deep-frying . The oil should be medium hot. To check if the oil is medium hot, drop a bit of tikki mixture into the oil; it should come up but not change colour right away. Drop 3-4 tikkis at a time into the oil depending upon the size of your vessel. Deep fry them on medium heat till they turn golden brown and crispy.

For serving, place 2 tikkis on a serving plate. Top the tikkis with 2-3 tablespoons of whisked yogurt. Pour mint chutney and tamarind chutney according to taste. Scatter some chopped onions. Sprinkle about ¼ teaspoon of chaat masala, ¼ teaspoon of roasted cumin powder and a pinch of red chilli powder. Garnish with pomegranate seeds.

Follow the same procedure for the remaining tikkis.

Serve immediately.

Recipe Tips:

Please make sure that the **yogurt you are using is not sour** as it will not taste good. You can use Greek yogurt whisked with little water or regular yogurt which is not sour.

To boil the potatoes, add 2 medium-sized potatoes along with 2 cups of water in a pressure cooker. Pressure cook on high for 4-5 whistles. Let the steam escape before opening the lid of pressure cooker. They can also be boiled in an **Instant Pot** for 10 minutes on high pressure with natural pressure release. You can also boil them in a **saucepan** until done.

Tamarind sauce/chutney can be bought from any Indian store or Asian section of most supermarkets.

Accompaniments

MANGO LASSI

 **10 MINS** |

Mango Lassi is a creamy and refreshing yogurt based drink that is quick and easy to prepare. I love making this lassi using fresh Indian mangoes when they are in season but you can also use tinned mango pulp if you can't get your hands on fresh mangoes.

Ingredients:

1 cup greek yogurt

1 cup kesar mango pulp
(tinned or fresh)

4-5 ice cubes

¼ teaspoon cardamom
powder (optional)

1 tablespoon finely chopped
fresh mango for
garnishing (optional)

1 mint sprig for garnishing
(optional)

Makes: 2-3 servings

Method:

Combine the yogurt, mango pulp and cardamom powder (if using) in an electric blender. Blend for a minute or till it becomes smooth and frothy.

Add the ice cubes and blend for few seconds.

Pour the lassi into glasses.

Garnish with finely chopped fresh mango and a mint sprig.

Serve immediately.

Recipe Tips:

I highly recommend using Greek yogurt as it makes the lassi thick & creamy. If using regular yogurt, please make sure that the yogurt is not sour otherwise the lassi won't taste good.

If the lassi is too thick for you, you can add ¼ cup milk and blend it for another 30 seconds.

Kesar mango (variety of Indian mango) is most suitable for making mango lassi as it imparts a bright yellow colour and a distinct flavour. However, if it's not available; you can use any other variety of mangoes.

I do not like to add sugar as the sweetness of the mangoes is enough to make a mildly sweet lassi with rich mango flavour. However, if you would like your lassi to be sweeter, you can add some sugar according to your taste.

CUCUMBER RAITA

 **10 MINS** |

Raita is a side-dish in Indian cuisine made by mixing yogurt with vegetables, herbs and spices. Cucumber Raita is cooling & refreshing raita that makes a perfect accompaniment with spicy curries or rice dishes like Biryani & Pulao.

Ingredients:

1 cup grated cucumber

1.5 cups whisked greek yogurt (chilled)

¼ cup water

1 tablespoon finely chopped mint leaves

½ teaspoon black salt or to taste

1 teaspoon roasted cumin powder

¼ teaspoon chaat masala (optional)

Makes: 3-4 servings

Method:

Combine all the ingredients in a bowl and mix well.

Keep it in the refrigerator till you are ready to serve.

Recipe Tips:

I like to use **greek yogurt** for this recipe as it makes the raita creamy and it's not sour. However, you can **replace it with regular yogurt** as long as it is not sour. You do not need to add water if you are using regular yogurt.

To make roasted cumin powder, roast cumin seeds in a flat pan on medium heat till they turn dark brown in colour (while stirring constantly). Turn off the heat and take them out in a dish. Cumin seeds get roasted very quickly so be careful not to burn them. Let the roasted cumin seeds cool to room temperature. Grind them in a spice grinder or in a mortar and pestle. Store in an air-tight jar and use as required.

GREEN APPLE & MINT CHUTNEY

 **10 MINS** |

Green Apple & Mint Chutney (commonly known as green chutney) is a simple and versatile dip that pairs perfectly with samosas, fritters, kebabs and other snacks. It also makes a great spread for wraps and sandwiches. There are different ways of making this chutney. The green apple can be replaced with raw mango. Some people like to add some fresh coriander as well to this chutney and some others like to serve it after mixing some yogurt in it. Whatever way you choose to make it; you are going to love this chutney.

Ingredients:

1 green apple

2 cups fresh mint leaves

1 large onion

1-2 green chillies (optional)

1 teaspoon chopped ginger

2 tablespoons freshly
     squeezed lemon juice

1 tablespoon sugar

½ teaspoon black salt

Salt to taste

Makes: 5-6 servings

Method:

Combine all the ingredients in an electric grinder/blender and grind till smooth. Add 1 or 2 tablespoons of water if it's not wet enough to grind. Do not add too much water.

Take the chutney out in a glass jar and keep refrigerated. This chutney can be kept in the refrigerator for up to a week.

MANGO CHUTNEY

 **10 MINS** | **12-15 MINS** | **GF** **VE**

Raw mango chunks simmered with sugar and flavourful spices to prepare a sweet, spicy and tangy relish which is definitely going to delight your taste buds. If you enjoy eating mango chutney with poppadoms in Indian restaurants, you would love this homemade version and wonder why you didn't prepare it before!

Ingredients:

- 2 cups finely chopped raw mangos
- ½ teaspoon red chilli powder or to taste
- ¼ teaspoon turmeric powder
- ¼ teaspoon asafoetida
- 4 tablespoons sugar or to taste
- 1.5 teaspoons salt or to taste
- ¼ teaspoon garam masala

Makes: 8-10 servings

Method:

Add the chopped raw mangoes, sugar, salt, asafoetida, red chilli powder and turmeric powder in a pan. Cook on medium heat, stirring continuously for 4-5 minutes. At this point, water will seep out of the raw mangoes.

Cover the pan and cook on low heat for 5-7 minutes or until it gets a thick chutney-like consistency. Add garam masala and mix well.

Keep it aside and let it cool. Once cooled, store it in a glass jar and keep refrigerated.

Recipe Tips:

This chutney keeps well in the refrigerator for 3-4 weeks.

You can adjust the amount of sugar according to your taste and the sourness of mangoes.

Please note that asafoetida is **naturally gluten-free** but some manufacturers sell it mixed with wheat flour. Please **check the ingredients** carefully if you are following a gluten-free diet.

Desserts

KESAR-PISTA KULFI

 **15 MINS |**

Rich and flavourful Indian ice-cream traditionally prepared by simmering milk till it becomes thick and almost half of its original quantity. I have come up with an easy and no-cook recipe. The result is equally divine without you having to spend long time in the kitchen. Hope you enjoy it.

Ingredients:

250 ml (1 cup) double cream

180 ml or ¾ cup condensed milk

½ teaspoon saffron (kesar)

2 tablespoons milk

2-3 tablespoons pistachios

½ teaspoon cardamom powder

1 teaspoon kewra water (optional)

Makes: 5-6 (Depending on the size of Kulfi Moulds)

Method:

Take 2 tablespoons milk in a microwaveable bowl and heat it for 30 seconds. Add the saffron strands to it and keep aside.

Coarsely grind half of the pistachios in a grinder. Keep aside. Chop the remaining pistachios and keep them for garnishing at the time of serving.

Place the double cream in the freezer for 10-15 minutes. It might be a good idea to chill your bowl and the beaters as well. Chilled cream whips up quicker and stays whipped for longer.

Chill the condensed milk in the freezer for 15 minutes or place it in the refrigerator for 3-4 hours.

After chilling the double cream and the equipment, beat it using a hand or electric whisk until soft peaks are formed.

Add the chilled condensed milk, milk with saffron strands, coarsely ground pistachios, cardamom powder and kewra water to the whipped cream. Mix gently using a spatula until just combined. Do not over mix.

Pour this mixture into the kulfi moulds and freeze for 8 hours or overnight . You can also use disposable glasses or paper cups covered with aluminium foil if you do not have kulfi moulds.

To serve, roll the kulfi moulds between your hands or keep under warm water for few seconds and turn out onto the plates. Garnish with chopped pistachios.

MANGO CHEESECAKE
(No-Bake)

PREP TIME 30 MINS | **Setting Time: 6+3 HRS**

An utterly delicious cheesecake with buttery biscuit base, mango cheesecake filling and mango jelly on the top. The refreshing fruity flavour and silky smooth texture makes it truly indulgent & divine.

Ingredients:

Biscuit Base

250g oats biscuits or digestives
2 tablespoons unsalted melted butter

Cream Cheese Layer

300g cream cheese
150 ml double cream or whipping cream
1 tablespoon gelatine powder
½ cup icing sugar
1 teaspoon vanilla extract
½ cup (125ml) mango pulp
1 large ripe mango, peeled & chopped

Mango Jelly Layer (Topmost)

½ cup (125ml) mango pulp
3-4 tablespoons icing sugar
1 tablespoon gelatine powder

Garnishing

½ large ripe mango, sliced
A mint sprig

Makes: 8 servings

Method:

Biscuit Base

To prepare the base of cheesecake, grind the biscuits into fine crumbs in a food processor. Melt the butter and combine it with the biscuits crumbs in a large bowl. Mix well.

Place the base of a spring foam cake tin upside down and line it with a square baking sheet so that there are overhangs on the sides. Both these steps will help in unmolding the cake easily once it is ready.

Spoon the biscuits-butter mixture in the cake tin and press firmly with the help of a potato masher or spatula to make an even base for the cheesecake. Keep it in the fridge for 30-40 minutes to set firmly.

Cream Cheese Layer

Place the whipping cream in the freezer for 10-15 minutes. It might be a good idea to chill your bowl and the beaters as well. Chilled cream whips up quicker and stays whipped for longer.

Whip the cream to stiff peaks using an electric whisk. Keep it aside.

In a separate bowl, combine cream cheese, icing sugar and vanilla essence. Mix well using an electric whisk till it becomes light and fluffy.

Add ½ cup of mango puree to the cream cheese mixture. Whisk again till well combined.

Take ½ cup hot water in a bowl. Add 1 tablespoon gelatine powder and stir well till the gelatine powder dissolves completely. Let it rest for 5 minutes. After letting the gelatine mixture rest for 5 minutes, add it (a little at a time) to the whisked cream cheese and mix well.

Add the cream cheese mixture to the whipped cream and fold it in the mixture till well combined. Do not overmix.

Pour half of the cream cheese mixture on the biscuit base. Scatter the chopped mango on it. Pour the remaining cream cheese mixture on top of scattered mangoes. Cover and refrigerate it for 6-8 hours or overnight to allow the cream cheese layer to set properly.

Mango Jelly Layer (Topmost)

Combine ¾ cup of mango pulp with 3-4 tablespoons of icing sugar (add more or less depending upon the sweetness of mango). Mix well using a whisk.

Take ½ cup hot water in a bowl. Add 1 tablespoon gelatine powder and stir well till the gelatine powder dissolves completely. Let it rest for 5 minutes. After letting the gelatine mixture rest for 5 minutes, add it to the mango pulp and mix well.

Gently pour the gelatine-mango pulp mixture over the cream cheese layer which was set in the refrigerator for 6-8 hours.

Cover and refrigerate for about 4 hours or till the mango pulp layer sets properly.

Unmolding & Garnishing

Release the sides of the springfoam cake tin by unlatching it. Slide the cheesecake onto a serving plate by holding it from the overhanging baking paper. Then slide the baking paper out from under the cheesecake.

Garnish with mango slices and a sprig of mint.

Recipe Tips:

Dip the knife in warm water and wipe it with a kitchen towel to cut neat pieces of cheese cake.

You can also use individual pudding pots or jars for this cheese cake.

"

Booked this cooking class with
Tanu for my sister as a gift for her
birthday, we had quite strict dietary
requirements which she catered for
amazingly.
    Thank you so much, my sister
loved the class and the food

Eda and Sid

"

GAJAR HALWA

 **15 MINS** | **25 MINS** | **GF** **V**

Classic Indian dessert primarily made of carrots, milk & sugar. It is quite popular in North India during winters. I have many childhood memories attached to this dessert. My mom used to prepare a big batch of this halwa and keep it in the refrigerator during the winter months. I used to relish it as a post-meal dessert and as a snack in-between the meals which I could quickly warm-up and eat.

Ingredients:

700g grated carrots (3 cups)

3 cups (750 ml) whole milk

2 tablespoons ghee

¾ cup (150g) granulated white sugar

½ teaspoon cardamom powder

1 tablespoon chopped almonds

1 tablespoon chopped pistachios

1 tablespoon chopped cashew nuts

Makes: 4 servings

Method:

Heat milk in a broad heavy-bottomed pan (preferably non-stick) and bring it to a boil. Keep stirring occasionally to prevent it from sticking to the bottom of the pan. Add grated carrots and cook on medium heat while stirring occasionally.

When the mixture starts thickening, reduce the heat to low and cook (while stirring very often) for another 8-10 minutes or till the mixture has almost dried. Keep scraping the sides of the pan (thickened milk gets stuck to it) and mix it with the carrot-milk mixture.

Add sugar and mix well. Cook for another 3-4 minutes while stirring continuously.

Add ghee and cardamom powder. Cook for another 3-4 minutes while stirring continuously.

Mix in the chopped nuts and save some for garnishing.

Serve warm garnished with nuts.

Recipe Tips:

The amount of sugar depends on taste. The quantity of sugar mentioned in this recipe will make halwa of mild sweetness. Add more sugar if you like a sweeter taste.

RASMALAI TRES LECHES CAKE

 **30 MINS** | **Baking Time: 25 MINS**

A **fusion dessert** that can be a show stopper for your next dinner party or any special occasion. **Tres Leches** is a sponge cake soaked in three kinds of milk: evaporated milk, condensed milk and heavy cream. I have replaced the heavy cream with whole milk to make it lighter and given it the flavour of a classic Indian dessert- **Rasmalai**. If you love moist cakes and Indian sweets, this is definitely going to become your favourite dessert.

Ingredients:

Cake
1 cup self-raising flour (120g)
1 cup (200g) granulated sugar
1 cup (225g) soft butter
3 tablespoons corn flour
4 eggs
1 teaspoon vanilla extract
½ teaspoon cardamom powder
½ teaspoon rose essence

Rasmalai Flavoured Milk
1.5 cups (375ml) evaporated milk
½ cup (125ml) condensed milk
½ cup (125ml) whole milk
8-10 strands of saffron
½ teaspoon cardamom powder
1 tablespoon ground pistachios
1 teaspoon kewra water (optional)

Frosting
300ml whipping cream
4 tablespoons icing sugar
½ teaspoon vanilla extract

Garnishing
Finely chopped pistachios
7-8 saffron strands
1 tablespoon dried rose petals

Method:

Sponge Cake

Pre -heat the oven to 180 degrees C (170 degrees C for fan ovens). Grease a 10x7 inch baking dish generously with butter.

Take soft butter (not melted) in a large mixing bowl. Add granulated sugar. Whisk the butter & sugar using an electric whisk till it looks pale and fluffy.

Beat the eggs (one at a time) in this mixture using an electric whisk. Add the vanilla extract, rose essence and cardamom powder along with the last egg. Beat the eggs until they are well combined in the mixture. Avoid over-mixing.

Sift the self-raising flour & corn flour into the mixture and mix well using a spatula. Mix till the flour is well combined and you can't see any dry flour. Please do not over-mix.

Add this batter to the prepared baking dish.

Bake at 180 degrees C (170 degrees C for fan ovens) for 20 - 25 minutes or until a skewer inserted in the centre comes out clean.

Rasmalai Flavoured Milk

To prepare the milk, bring ½ cup of whole milk to a sharp boil in a saucepan. Switch off the heat and add the saffron strands. Cover the saucepan and keep aside for 10 minutes. After 10 minutes, add the condensed milk, evaporated milk, kewra water, cardamom powder and ground pistachios to the saffron milk. Mix well and keep aside to let it cool.

Once the cake is baked, poke holes all over the cake with a skewer while it's still hot.

Pour the prepared milk all over the cake so that it covers the entire cake evenly.

Cover it with kitchen foil or cling film and place in the refrigerator for 4-5 hours or overnight.

Place the cream in the freezer for 10-15 minutes before whipping.

Frosting

To prepare the frosting, add the chilled cream and 3-4 tablespoons of icing sugar in a large mixing bowl. Whip the cream using an electric whisk. Start with low speed and then go on high till the cream looks almost whipped (around 2-3 minutes). Whip on low speed in the end until stiff peaks form.

Transfer the whipped cream to a piping bag fitted with an open star tip (I used Wilton #1M). Pipe the frosting on the entire cake.

Garnishing

Top with finely chopped pistachios, saffron strands and dried rose petals.

Cut into large squares and serve with the prepared saffron & pistachio milk.

Recipe Tips:

Make sure all the ingredients for the sponge cake batter are at room temperature.

Do not replace soft butter with melted butter. If you forget to keep the butter out of the refrigerator, cut it into small cubes and microwave it on defrost setting for 20 seconds or till it softens.

If in a hurry, you can neatly spread a thick layer of whipped cream on the cake using a spoon or frosting spatula.

Variation:

For making **Rose Tres Leches Cake**, replace the kewra water, saffron and cardamom powder with 4 tablespoons of rose-syrup while preparing the milk to be poured on the cake.

Rose Syrup can be bought from any Indian store or online.

I live in Turkey and always crave for Indian food especially Indian street food. Then I found Tanu's Indian cooking classes and contacted her for online classes. I never thought of cooking Indian street food at home but after taking her classes I am confidently preparing it at home.

Farhana

SOOJI HALWA

 **5 MINS** | **15 MINS** | **V**

Simple Indian dessert prepared using very basic ingredients - semolina, sugar & ghee. In India, it is commonly prepared on religious occasions as Prasad (offering to God). This is another dessert that takes me back to my childhood days. Whenever I craved for something sweet, my grandmother would prepare this in her small kadai (a bowl-shaped frying pan with two handles used in Indian cooking) and come out of the kitchen like a magician in literally 15 minutes. My recipe is a less sweeter version of my grandmother's recipe. You can increase the quantity of sugar if you like a sweeter halwa.

Ingredients:

1 cup fine semolina

¾ cup ghee + 1 tablespoon

¾ cup sugar

½ teaspoon cardamom powder

2 tablespoons chopped nuts (almonds, cashew nuts & pistachios)

2 tablespoons black raisins

Method:

Heat 1 tablespoon ghee in a pan. Add the raisins and sauté them on medium heat for 1-2 minutes or till they swell up slightly. Remove them from the pan and keep aside.

Add the chopped nuts in the same pan and roast them lightly on medium heat. Keep stirring continuously as the nuts can burn very quickly. Once roasted, remove from the pan and keep aside.

Heat ¾ cup ghee in the same pan. Add semolina and sauté on low-medium heat. Roast the semolina in ghee while stirring continuously. Sauté for around 7-8 minutes on low-medium heat or till it becomes fragrant and change colour to light golden brown.

When the semolina is roasted, add cardamom powder and sugar. Mix well.

Add 3 cups of water and mix well. Be careful as the water will bubble. Once it starts bubbling, reduce the heat to lowest setting.

Keep stirring continuously so that there are no lumps. Stir for 2-3 minutes or till the halwa thickens and leaves the sides of the pan.

Add the roasted chopped nuts and raisins (saving some for garnishing). Mix well.

Serve warm garnished with some more nuts.

ROSE FALOODA

 **20 MINS** | **V**

Refreshing summer dessert drink which is a treat for the taste-buds as well as the eyes. Traditionally, the milk used in falooda is simmered on low heat until it becomes thick and creamy. I have used the ready evaporated milk in this recipe which makes it quick and hassle-free.

Ingredients:

500 ml evaporated milk (chilled)

5 tablespoons rose syrup or to taste

1 tablespoon basil seeds

½ cup or a handful of falooda sev

3 kesar-pista kulfis (page 129) or 3 scoops of vanilla ice cream

2 teaspoons kewra water

1 tablespoon chopped pistachios

1 tablespoon sliced almonds

8-10 ice-cubes

Makes: 2-3 servings (Depending on the size of glasses)

Method:

Take ½ cup (120ml) water in a bowl. Add the basil seeds and keep aside for 15 minutes.

Take 3 cups water in a separate bowl. Add 2 teaspoons of kewra water and mix well. Add 8-10 ice-cubes and keep aside.

Boil the falooda sev in water for 3-4 minutes or according to the instructions on the pack. Drain the sev and rinse them with cold water. Add them in the bowl containing iced water.

To assemble the falooda, take a tall glass. First add the falooda sev and then add 1 tablespoon of soaked basil seeds. Drizzle 1 tablespoon of rose syrup. Do not mix the layers.

Add the chilled evaporated milk till the glass is about ¾th full leaving enough space for a kulfi or a scoop of ice-cream. Add the kulfi or ice-cream. Drizzle 1 teaspoon of rose-syrup on the top. Garnish with nuts.

Serve immediately.

Recipe Tips:

If preparing for guests or a special occasion, you can keep all the ingredients ready and assemble them in glasses just before serving.

The basil seeds can be replaced by chia seeds.

Acknowledgements

Writing this book has been a great pleasure, a true labour of love. It was way too harder and time-consuming than I thought and I couldn't have done it without some people I have been blessed with in my life or came across during my book writing journey.

Huge thanks to my husband, Ravi who is my rock and has always been a huge support since I started following my passion. Thank you for believing in me even more than I do. Thank you for waiting patiently for the meals till I was done with the photographs, rushing to the supermarket when I ran short of ingredients, calming me down whenever I got overwhelmed with all the work and the list goes on.... Thank you for everything!

Another person who has always inspired me to bring the best out of me is my best friend, Shweta. She has always been by my side in spite of being miles apart from me. I do not have words to thank her...I couldn't have done it without her.

I would also like to thank all the wonderful people who attended my cooking classes, tried and tested my recipes and gave me valuable feedback.

I would fail in my duty if I do not thank the interior-designer of this book, Marigold who worked day and night with me. The book wouldn't have appeared in the shape it is now without her efforts.

Special thanks to my parents without whom I wouldn't have reached where I am today. Heartfelt thanks to my Mumma who has always been my inspiration in the kitchen and in my life; I hope she is watching from somewhere.

I am also thankful to the rest of my family and friends who always appreciated my food and encouraged me to follow my passion.

Printed in Great Britain
by Amazon